Church and Sacraments

faith first

Legacy Edition

RCL Benziger

Cincinnati, Ohio

This book reflects the new revision of the

ROMAN MISSAL

THIRD EDITION

"The Ad Hoc Committee to Oversee the Use of the Catechism, United States Conference of Catholic Bishops, has found this catechetical series, copyright 2006, to be in conformity with the *Catechism of the Catholic Church*."

NIHIL OBSTAT
Rev. Msgr. Robert M. Coerver
Censor Librorum

IMPRIMATUR
† Most Rev. Charles V. Grahmann
Bishop of Dallas

September 1, 2004

The Nihil Obstat and Imprimatur are official declarations that the material reviewed is free of doctrinal or moral error. No implication is contained therein that those granting the Nihil Obstat and Imprimatur agree with the contents, opinions, or statements expressed.

Send all inquiries to:
RCL Benziger
8805 Governor's Hill Drive
Suite 400
Cincinnati, Ohio 45249

Toll Free   877-275-4725
Fax   800-688-8356

Visit us at www.RCLBenziger.com
            www.FaithFirst.com

20469   ISBN 978-0-7829-1070-4 (Student Book)
20489   ISBN 978-0-7829-1082-7 (Catechist Guide)
20528   ISBN 978-0-7829-1113-8 (Teacher Guide)

Manufactured for RCL Benziger in Cincinnati, OH,

ACKNOWLEDGMENTS
Scripture excerpts are taken or adapted from the *New American Bible with Revised New Testament and Psalms* Copyright © 1991, 1986, 1970, Confraternity of Christian Doctrine, Washington, DC. Used with permission. All rights reserved. No part of the *New American Bible* may be reproduced by any means without the permission of the copyright owner.

Excerpts are taken or adapted from the *Rite of Baptism for Children* © 1969, International Commission on English in the Liturgy, Inc. (ICEL); the English translation of the *Roman Missal* © 2010, ICEL; the English translation of the Act of Contrition from *Rite of Penance* © 1974, ICEL; the English translation of *The Ordination of Deacons, Priests, and Bishops* © 1975, ICEL; the English translation of *A Book of Prayers* © 1982, ICEL; the English translation of *A Book of Blessings* © 1988 ICEL; *Catholic Household Blessings and Prayers* (revised edition) © 2007, United States Conference of Catholic Bishops, Washington, D.C. All rights reserved.

Excerpts are taken or adapted from English translation of *Kyrie Eleison, Nicene Creed, Apostles' Creed, Sanctus and Benedictus, Agnus Dei, Gloria Patri,* and *Te Deum Laudamus* by the International Consultation on English Texts (ICET).

Photo and Art Credits appear on page 152.

Faith First Legacy Edition
Development Team

Developing a religion program requires the gifts and talents of many individuals working together as a team. RCL Benziger is proud to acknowledge the contributions of these dedicated people.

Program Theology Consultants
Reverend Louis J. Cameli, S.T.D.
Reverend Robert D. Duggan, S.T.D.

Advisory Board
Judith Deckers, M.Ed.
Elaine McCarron, SCN, M.Div.
Marina Herrera, Ph.D.
Reverend Frank McNulty, S.T.D.
Reverend Ronald J. Nuzzi, Ph.D.

National Catechetical Advisor
Jacquie Jambor

Catechetical Specialist
Jo Rotunno

Contributing Writers
Student Book & Catechist/Teacher Guides
Christina DeCamp
Judith Deckers
Mary Beth Jambor
Eileen A. McGrath
Reverend Robert D. Duggan
Reverend Steven M. Lanza
Michele Norfleet

Art & Design Director	*Electronic Page Makeup*	*Production Director*
Lisa Brent	Laura Fremder	Jenna Nelson

Designers/Photo Research	*Project Editors*	*Web Site Producers*
Pat Bracken	Patricia A. Classick	Joseph Crisalli
Kristy O. Howard	Steven M. Ellair	Demere Henson
Susan Smith	Ronald C. Lamping	

General Editor	*President/Publisher*
Ed DeStefano	Maryann Nead

Contents

Welcome to Faith First

Welcome to **Faith First: Church and Sacraments**. This book invites you to explore the mystery of the Church. The Church is the gathering of the People of God who profess faith in the Incarnate Son of God, Jesus Christ, and live today empowered by the Holy Spirit. You will learn more about what it means to take responsibility for being a member of the Body of Christ and continuing Christ's work on earth. You will gain deeper insight into the ways that prayer and the sacraments bind you more closely to Christ and the Body of Christ, the Church, and empower you to live your Christian life more fully.

You will learn more of the story of Saint Paul the Apostle, whose energy and great faith in the Risen Christ moved him to spread the Gospel throughout the Mediterranean world. You will rediscover the fascinating story of Nicodemus, who pursued Jesus with his questions and was awakened to faith through the power of the Holy Spirit. The knowledge you gain about the Church and the sacraments will only bear fruit and make a difference in your life if you cooperate with the grace of the Holy Spirit. So, let's get started and explore more deeply the story of God's people.

Church and Sacraments

Beginning Reflections

Jesus, the Incarnate Son of God and Savior of the world, lived and died on earth, was buried and raised from the dead, and returned to his Father in glory. The glorified Lord lives today in the Church. In the weeks ahead you will come to know more about the Church. You will discuss that the Church is the new People of God, the Body of Christ, and the Temple of the Holy Spirit. You will deepen your understanding of how we are made sharers in the Passion, death, Resurrection, and glorious Ascension of Jesus Christ through the celebration of the sacraments.

Through Baptism you are joined to Christ, receive the gift of the Holy Spirit, and become a member of the Church. The Holy Spirit invites you to take part in the life and work of the Church. Consider the following reflections. Jot down your initial responses. This reflection time will help you open your mind and heart to experience the grace and power of the Holy Spirit, who lives within you and within the whole Church.

Through Baptism you were joined to Christ and became a member of the Body of Christ, the Church.

I will follow Christ, the Head of the Church, more faithfully by

_____

_____

_____ .

Make a point to be present and to participate fully and consciously in the celebration of Sunday Mass.

Listening attentively to the Scripture readings and sharing in the Eucharist regularly helps me grow as a member of the Church by

_____

_____

_____ .

Renew your habit of daily prayer. Spend a few moments at the beginning of each day, at regular times throughout the day, and at the end of each day.

Daily prayer keeps me in touch with Jesus by

_____

_____

_____ .

Participate in all class sessions. Ask questions that will help you grow closer to Christ.

Making a sincere effort to learn more about the Church and the sacraments could result in

_____

_____

_____ .

Imagine how you will participate in the life of the Church when you are older.

I can begin to learn and prepare for that work now. One specific way I can do this is by

_____

_____ .

UNIT ONE
The Church

What is the Church?

Getting Ready

The Church

What do you already know about the Catholic Church?

_____

_____

_____

_____

_____

_____

_____

_____

_____

Questions I Have

What questions about the Catholic Church do you hope these chapters will answer?

_____

_____

_____

_____

_____

Faith Vocabulary

Put an X next to the faith vocabulary terms that you know. Put a ? next to the faith vocabulary terms that you need to know more about.

_____ apostolic succession

_____ Body of Christ

_____ Communion of Saints

_____ consecrated life

_____ devotions

_____ ecumenism

_____ infallibility

_____ laypeople

_____ Magisterium

_____ missionary

_____ ordained ministry

_____ People of God

_____ prayer of contemplation

_____ prayer of meditation

A Scripture Story

Saint Paul the Apostle departing from Caesarea on his third missionary journey

How did Saint Paul the Apostle spread the Gospel?

The Church: The People of God

1

FAITH FOCUS

Why do we call the Church the new People of God?

FAITH VOCABULARY

Church

Communion of Saints

laypeople

ordained ministry

consecrated life

To what groups do you belong? Why do you belong to those groups?

Having friends and belonging to groups is important to all people—young and old. "Belonging" just seems to be part of who we are.

Everyone who is baptized belongs to the Church. We become part of the worldwide faith community of Catholics, members of the Body of Christ and heirs of salvation. No member of the Church is ever really alone. Our faith unites us.

What does it mean to you to belong to the Church?

World Youth Day, 2002, Toronto, Canada

[G]race to you and peace from God our Father and the Lord Jesus Christ.

EPHESIANS 1:2

The Plan of God

The **Church** is the sign and instrument of salvation. It is the sign and instrument of our reconciliation and communion with God and with one another. The origin of the Church lies deep within the plan of God from the very beginning of time. It was the design of God in creation to share his own divine life with those he created and to "call together in a holy Church those who should believe in Christ" (*Constitution on the Church* 2).

Pentecost,
stained glass

God promised to Noah a universal covenant with all people (see Genesis 9:9–13). Next God promised Abraham that he would be the father of a great nation (see Genesis 12:2). This foreshadowed the future gathering of all nations into one people. God elected the people of Israel to be his people. He entered the Covenant with them on Mount Sinai and gave his Law to them through Moses. Later the prophets announced that God would make a new and everlasting covenant (see Jeremiah 31:31–34) with all people—just as he had promised.

The New and Everlasting Covenant

The promise of the new Covenant was instituted in Jesus Christ (see Luke 22:14–20). Jesus called his first followers, who became known as the Twelve, to be the foundation of this new People of God. When his redemptive work was accomplished on earth, the Risen and glorified Christ returned to his Father in heaven. As Jesus promised, the Father sent the Holy Spirit in his name. It is the Holy Spirit who forms the followers of Jesus into the new People of God, the Church.

It is God's plan that all people belong to the new People of God. In the new dispensation of the Holy Spirit, acceptance of the Church is inseparable from belief in God.

The Church is on pilgrimage until the end of time. Then all God's children will be gathered together in fulfillment of his plan. The Church will be the shining Bride of Christ (see Revelation 22:17). There will be "one flock, one shepherd" (John 10:16).

Why is the Church called the new People of God?

The Communion of Saints

The Church is also known as the **Communion of Saints.** The Communion of Saints is a communion of holy things and holy people that make up the Church.

A Communion of Holy Things

There is a deep solidarity among the people that God has made holy by sharing his life with us. The Church is a:

- **communion in the faith.**
  There is a sharing in the faith handed down from the Apostles.
- **communion in the sacraments.**
  There is a sharing in the Paschal Mystery that binds us to one another in the Lord Jesus.
- **communion in the Holy Spirit.**
  The Church shares and is enriched by spiritual gifts of the Holy Spirit (see 1 Corinthians 12:4–11).
- **communion of charity, or love.**
  After explaining that the greatest spiritual gift is love, Saint Paul writes, "[S]eek to have an abundance of [spiritual gifts] for building up the church" (1 Corinthians 14:12). Love binds us together.

A Communion of Holy People

The Church is also a community, or communion, of holy people. This communion of holy people includes:

- the faithful on earth,
- the faithful who are being purified after death in purgatory,
- the faithful in heaven.

The Church on earth continues to pray for those being purified after their bodily death. The saints living in heaven care about us and care for us. They serve the faithful on earth as our intercessors before God in heaven. This faith moves us to pray to them and to learn about their lives on earth.

Did you Know...

The word *Jerusalem* means "the foundation of God" or "city of peace." On earth the city of Jerusalem is the center of God's people, the earthly foundation of his people. In the Book of Revelation, the "new Jerusalem" is not a city. It is the fulfillment of God's plan when all creation is founded on him, living in peace and communion with him and one another.

The Book of Genesis begins with the creation of the world. The last book of the Bible, Revelation, tells of the new creation of all things in Christ.

FAITH CONNECTION

Design or describe an image that illustrates the Communion of Saints.

The People of the Church

The visible Church on earth is made up of many people. Each has responsibility for the work, or mission, of the Church. Joined to Christ in Baptism, all the baptized are called to share in the Paschal Mystery of Christ's Passion, death, Resurrection, and glorious Ascension and to be happy with him forever. This is the vocation, or calling, of all Christians.

The Holy Spirit blesses the People of God with charisms, or talents and gifts and responsibilities to live that vocation and to help build up the Body of Christ on earth. Saint Paul the Apostle wrote:

There are different kinds of spiritual gifts but the same Spirit; there are different forms of service but the same Lord; there are different workings but the same God who produces all of them in everyone. To each individual the manifestation of the Spirit is given for some benefit. I CORINTHIANS 12:4–7

Laypeople

At Baptism all the newly baptized receive the gift of the Holy Spirit and are anointed with the blessed oil called chrism. The presider prays:

He [God the Father] now anoints you with the chrism of salvation, so that, united with his people, you may remain for ever a member of Christ who is Priest, Prophet, and King.

FROM RITE OF BAPTISM

After their anointing the newly baptized receive a lighted candle, a symbol of Christ. They are to live as lights of Christ in the world.

Most of the baptized are members of the laity, or **laypeople.** Laypeople are all the members of the Church who have not been ordained as a bishop, priest, or deacon or who have not taken vows or promises to live the consecrated life as a member of a religious community. Laypeople are lights of faith, hope, and love in their families and among their friends, in their communities, in their workplaces, and in their parishes. They are living witnesses for Christ at the very heart of the human community.

Explain how laypeople live their vocation as members of the People of God.

Neophytes, or newly initiated members of the Church

Ordained Ministers

Bishops, priests, and deacons are members of the **ordained ministry** of the Church. They are ordained to serve the whole Church. Through the ordained ministry, especially of bishops and priests, the presence of Christ as Head of the Church is made visible in the midst of the Church. Bishops are helped by priests, their coworkers, and by deacons in their work of teaching the faith, celebrating divine worship, and guiding the faithful entrusted to their care. All ordained ministers of the Church are clergy.

The Consecrated Life

Laypeople and ordained ministers sometimes vow or promise to live lives of poverty, chastity, and obedience in a way of life approved by the Church. They can live out this **consecrated life** publicly in religious communities or even as cloistered religious, or religious who do not leave the place where they live, work, and pray. In whatever ways these members of the Church live out their vocation, they are living signs of God's saving love at work in the world. Their lives remind us to keep our focus on living the Gospel.

How do those in the ordained ministry and those in the consecrated life live out their baptismal promises?

The Pope and Other Bishops

Jesus gave his Church on earth a structure. He chose the Twelve with Saint Peter as their head to serve the Church in his name (see John 21:15–17). The pope is the successor of Saint Peter. The pope is also the bishop of Rome and the head of all the bishops. He is the vicar of Christ on earth and has been given the ministry to care for the whole Church. He is the visible foundation and pastor of the universal Church on earth. Bishops are the successors of the Apostles. Bishops are chosen by the pope to lead local churches in every part of the world. As the chief pastor for his local church, a bishop stands in the place of Christ.

Bishop as Teacher

The first duty of the bishop is to preach the Good News. Guided by the Holy Spirit, the bishop, as a successor of the Apostles, passes on, preserves, and defends the truth of the Gospel. He teaches authoritatively on matters of faith and morals. The faithful are called to believe what the Church teaches.

Bishop as Sanctifier

Helped by priests, their coworkers, and by deacons, bishops sanctify the Church by their prayers and work, by their ministry of word and sacrament, as well as by their personal example of holiness. Bishops have the responsibility and authority to see to it that the sacraments are celebrated reverently with the faithful in their care. Bishops are stewards of the grace of Christ, especially of the Eucharist over which they preside or delegate to priests as coworkers.

Bishop as Pastor

The bishop leads and serves the faithful by following the example of Christ the Good Shepherd (see Luke 22:26). Those chosen to shepherd the Church as bishops are to serve others as Jesus served (see John 13:14–17). They are the sign and source of the unity of the Church in the particular church they serve.

FAITH CONNECTION

Look up and read these Scripture passages. Describe what each teaches about the ministry of the leaders of the Church.

Matthew 20:25–28   *John 10:11–16*

_____   _____

_____   _____

_____   _____

OUR CHURCH
MAKES A DIFFERENCE

The Naming of a Pope

Catholics believe that the naming of a pope is the work of the Holy Spirit. It is by the work of the Holy Spirit working side by side and through the leaders of the Catholic Church that a pope, the successor of Saint Peter the Apostle, is chosen.

The choosing, or electing, of a pope takes place at a special gathering, or conclave, of the cardinals of the Church. The title cardinal is usually given to a bishop, although nonbishops have been named cardinals. Cardinals belong to the College of Cardinals and serve the Church by advising the pope and electing the pope.

Conclave of the College of Cardinals, 1978. Papal electors entering Sistine Chapel for the election of a new pope

Black smoke indicating a new pope has not been elected

Guidelines for Electing a Pope

The guidelines for electing a pope have changed over the years. The current guidelines include:

- No cardinal over eighty years old is eligible to elect a new pope.
- The maximum number of papal electors is 120.
- A two-thirds majority of votes is required.
- All voting is silent.
- The conclave takes place in the Sistine Chapel, Vatican City, Rome.

Electing a New Pope

When the papal electors enter the conclave, they take an oath to follow the rules of the conclave and obey the rules of secrecy about the voting and the discussions.

When a new pope is elected, the paper ballots are burned without a chemical additive. This creates white smoke—the sign to the crowds gathered in Saint Peter's Square and the whole world that a new pope has been elected. The newly elected pope appears on the balcony and gives his blessing to the world, as the crowds jubilantly shout, "Viva il Papa!" or "Long live the pope!"

Imagine that your class was given the opportunity to nominate one of the cardinals to be the pope. What qualities would you want the new pope to have?

White smoke indicating a new pope has been elected

15

WHAT DIFFERENCE
Does Faith Make in My Life?

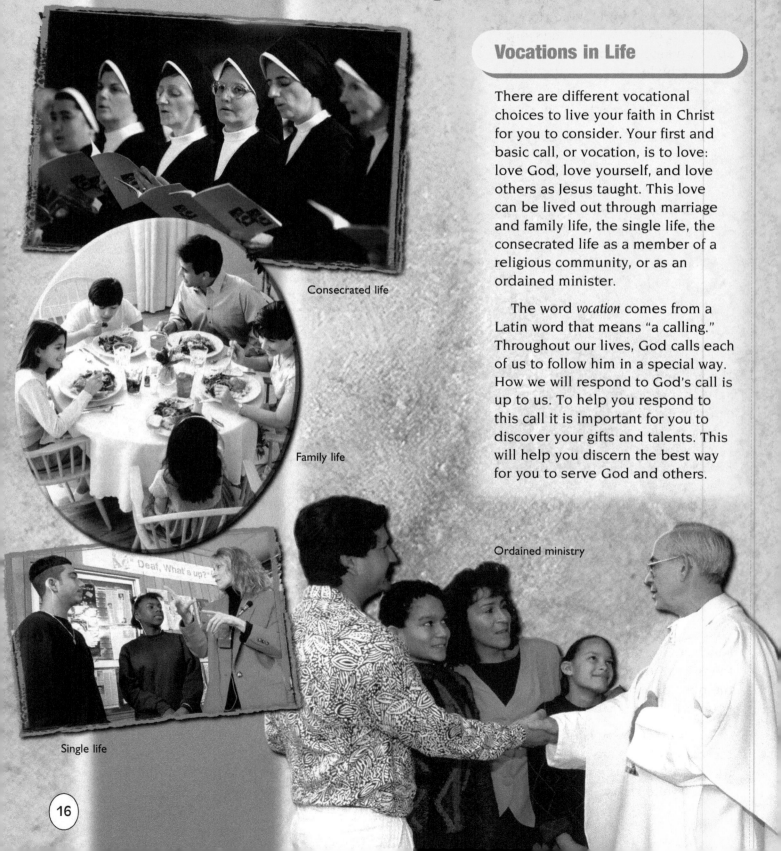

Consecrated life

Family life

Single life

Ordained ministry

Vocations in Life

There are different vocational choices to live your faith in Christ for you to consider. Your first and basic call, or vocation, is to love: love God, love yourself, and love others as Jesus taught. This love can be lived out through marriage and family life, the single life, the consecrated life as a member of a religious community, or as an ordained minister.

The word *vocation* comes from a Latin word that means "a calling." Throughout our lives, God calls each of us to follow him in a special way. How we will respond to God's call is up to us. To help you respond to this call it is important for you to discover your gifts and talents. This will help you discern the best way for you to serve God and others.

Discernment

Discernment is a prayerful way to gain insight into and to learn more about yourself, your gifts, and your skills, so you can recognize or determine your vocation in life. This is an ongoing process. It takes thought and prayer throughout your life. Here are a few steps to help you practice discernment.

- ◆ **Set aside time to be quiet.** Ask the Holy Spirit to open your mind and heart to what God is saying to you about your life.
- ◆ **Be open to different possibilities.** It is important to consider the possibility that God may be calling you to be ordained, to live in religious life, or to be single.

- ◆ **Talk to people.**
  —a married couple
  —a religious brother or sister
  —a deacon, priest, or bishop
  —a single person
- ◆ **Value your uniqueness.**
  —your personality
  —your gifts
  —your talents
  Think about the best way you can use your gifts and talents to live a holy life and share the goodness of God's love with others.
- ◆ **Remember that discernment is an ongoing process.** The more time you give to it, the better you will become at discovering who God is calling you to be.

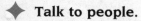
Faith Decision

- In small groups discuss how the discernment process can help you right now in your life.

- Imagine that your class is making a class quilt. What would you put in the square that would tell others about your gifts and qualities?

This week I will think about what God is calling me to do with my life. I will set aside some time to practice some of the steps of discernment. I will do this on

_____
                    (date)

from _____ to _____.
        (time)   *(time)*

PRAY and REVIEW

Prayer for Vocations

Leader:

God the Father calls each member of the Church to share in and continue the work of his Son. Let us listen to the word of God.

Reader 1:

A reading from the First Letter of Paul to the Corinthians. *Proclaim 1 Corinthians 12:27–31.* The word of the Lord.

All: Thanks be to God.

Leader:

Take a few moments to think about your gifts and talents. Ask yourself how God is calling you to use these blessings. *(Pause.)*

Lord God, we ask that we may know and follow the vocation to which you are calling us.

All: Lord, hear our prayer.

Reader 2:

We pray for those who serve your people as bishops, priests, and deacons.

All: Lord, hear our prayer.

Reader 3:

We pray for consecrated religious and for those who serve your people as single people.

All: Lord, hear our prayer.

Reader 4:

We pray for those who serve you as Christian married spouses and for their families.

All: Lord, hear our prayer.

Leader:

Lord God, Father of all, send faith-filled workers to continue the work of Christ, your Son. Send the Holy Spirit to be their helper and guide. We ask this through Christ our Lord.

All: Amen.

FAITH VOCABULARY

Define each of these faith terms:

1. Church
2. Communion of Saints
3. laypeople
4. ordained ministry
5. consecrated life

MAIN IDEAS

Choose either (a) or (b) from each set of items. Write a brief paragraph to answer each of your choices.

1. (a) Describe the Church as the new People of God.

   (b) Describe the role of laypeople in the Church.

2. (a) Explain the ministry of the pope and other bishops in the Church.

   (b) Describe the role in the Church of those who live the consecrated life.

CRITICAL THINKING

Using what you have learned in this chapter, reflect on and explain this statement:

The Church is both human and divine.

FAMILY DISCUSSION

How can our family be a sign that reminds others that God calls all people to be one family, the People of God?

For more ideas on ways your family can live your faith, visit the "Faith First for Families" page at **www.FaithFirst.com**. Also check out the Teen Center for additional activities.

The Church: The Body of Christ

2

FAITH FOCUS

How do images help us understand the mystery of the Church?

FAITH VOCABULARY

Body of Christ	Temple of the Holy Spirit
charisms	Marks of the Church
ecumenism	apostolic succession
Magisterium	infallibility

What things in life are a mystery to you?

Some situations are very difficult to understand or even seem to be beyond our understanding. Some problems seem too difficult to solve. We sometimes call such things mysteries. The Church is a mystery of faith.

Why do you think the Church is called a mystery?

World. Diana Ong (1940–), Chinese-American artist.

[There is] one Lord, one faith, one baptism; one God and Father of all.
EPHESIANS 4:5–6

The Mystery of the Church

A Mystery of Faith

We believe in many mysteries of faith. A mystery of faith is something we believe because God has revealed it and the Church teaches it. It is a truth of faith that we will never be able to understand fully, so vast is its meaning. No matter how much we learn about it, there will always be more than we can learn and understand about a mystery of faith.

One reason the Church is a mystery is that the Church is made up of both a visible, or human, reality and an invisible, or spiritual, reality. The Church is both a visible community with a hierarchical structure and an invisible spiritual communion that mirrors the unity of the Holy Trinity. The Church is both an earthly reality that exists here and now on earth and a reality that exists beyond time and space in heaven, where the Lord reigns in glory surrounded by all the saints.

From the days of the early Church, Christians have used images to describe the nature and work of the Church. Each image in its own way tells us a partial truth about the mystery of the Church.

Images of the Church

The Body of Christ and the Temple of the Holy Spirit are two images for the Church that are found in the New Testament.

The Body of Christ

The image of the **Body of Christ** compares the Church to the functioning of the human body. Saint Paul the Apostle writes:

> Now you are Christ's body, and individually parts of it.
>
> 1 CORINTHIANS 12:27

As the parts of a physical body are united one to another, so Christians are united with one another in Christ. Christ is "the head of the body, the church" (Colossians 1:18). Christ directs and gives life to us. Together we make up the "whole Christ."

Temple of the Holy Spirit

The image of the Church as the **Temple of the Holy Spirit** is used to describe the indwelling of the Holy Spirit in the Church and within the hearts of the faithful. Saint Paul used this image in his First Letter to the Corinthians (see 1 Corinthians 3:16 and 6:19). The Holy Spirit is the source of the richness of the Church's **charisms** (see 1 Corinthians 12:27–31). Charisms are special graces to be used "so that the church may be built up" (1 Corinthians 14:5).

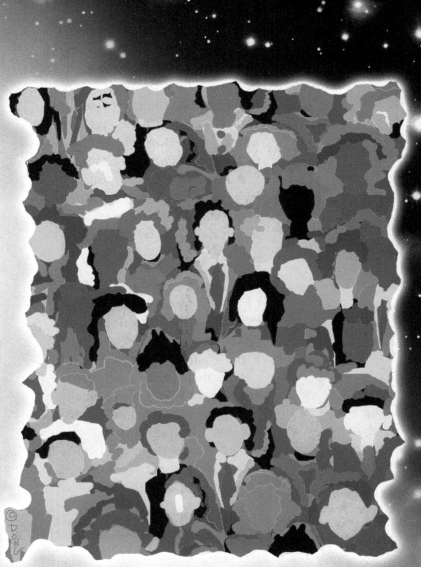

Family Plan. Diana Ong (1940–), Chinese-American artist.

FAITH CONNECTION

Choose either the image "Body of Christ" or "Temple of the Holy Spirit." Describe what it helps you understand about the Church. Share your ideas with a partner.

The Marks of the Church

Each Sunday at Mass you pray the Nicene Creed. You profess, "I believe . . . in one, holy, catholic and apostolic Church." One, holy, catholic, and apostolic are the four **Marks of the Church.** The Marks of the Church are the essential features of the Church founded by Jesus Christ. They help us understand the mystery and mission of the Church.

The Church Is One

The Church is the one Body of Christ. The visible bonds of unity that unite Christ's followers as "one" include:

- profession of one faith received from the Apostles;
- common worship, especially Baptism, the Eucharist, and the other sacraments; and
- direct succession of bishops from the Apostles through the sacrament of Holy Orders.

These bonds of unity within the Church are found most fully in the Catholic Church. Non-Catholic Christians who do not share fully with us in these bonds of unity today are joined to us "in some, although imperfect, communion" (*Decree on Ecumenism* 3). In these non-Catholic Christian communities, there are many elements of holiness and truth that are truly means of salvation for their members.

Jesus founded one Church. At the Last Supper, Jesus prayed:

> "[M]ay all be one, as you, Father, are in me and I in you, that they also may be in us, that the world may believe that you sent me."
> JOHN 17:21

All Christians must make Jesus' prayer their own prayer. We must pray and work for the restoration of the unity of the Church. We call this work of the Church **ecumenism.**

The Church Is Holy

The Church is holy because in Baptism we are joined to Christ, become adopted children of God the Father, and receive the gift of the Holy Spirit. We share in the life and love of God, the Holy One. We receive the grace to live a life of holiness.

How do the Marks "one" and "holy" help us understand the mystery of the Church?

Cardinal Idris Cassidy (left), President of the Pontifical Council for Promoting Christian Unity, and German Bishop Christian Kraus (right), President of the Lutheran World Federation

Blessed Pope John Paul II and Bartholomew I, Ecumenical Patriarch and Archbishop of Constantinople

Ordination of bishops

The Church Is Catholic

"Catholic" is the Mark of the Church that tells us that in God's plan all people are to become one People of God. The Church of Christ that we profess in the Nicene Creed to be "one, holy, catholic and apostolic" can be found in its fullest in the Catholic Church.

What about all those people who are not baptized? The Catholic Church believes and trusts and teaches that God's love has no limits. People who seek to follow God's will according to their conscience and who through no fault of their own do not come to faith in Christ and his Church can still achieve eternal salvation. Their salvation comes about as a result of the grace of Jesus Christ.

Through his death on the cross and his Resurrection, Christ has won forgiveness of sins and reconciliation with God for the entire human race. Jesus is "the way and the truth and the life" (John 14:6) in whom salvation is found. It is in this sense that the Church teaches that all salvation—even the salvation of the unbaptized—comes from Christ through his Body, the Church.

The Church Is Apostolic

Apostolic means "from the time of the Apostles." The Church has its origin and foundation in the life of the original Apostles whom Jesus chose to act in his name. Ever since that time, leadership in the Church has been handed down from Saint Peter and the other Apostles to the popes and bishops through the sacrament of Holy Orders. This connection of all popes and bishops back to Saint Peter and the first Apostles is called **apostolic succession.**

How do the Marks "catholic" and "apostolic" help us understand the mystery of the Church?

Since the days of the early Church, the Apostles and their successors have written letters to teach and guide the Church. This tradition still exists today. The writing of pastoral letters is one way the bishops of the United States, either individually or together as the United States Conference of Catholic Bishops (USCCB), instruct the faithful on Catholic teachings, worship, social concerns, and other topics that are important to the life of the Church.

Cardinals and bishops from around the world praying before a meeting at the Vatican

The Magisterium

The **Magisterium** is the living teaching authority and office of the Church, entrusted to the pope and the bishops by Christ. Jesus made Saint Peter the visible foundation, or rock, on which he would build the Church (see Matthew 16:18–19). Peter and his successors would be the "rock" and source of the unity of the Church founded by Jesus. The Church uses the term *College of Bishops* to name the unity of all the bishops (the successors of the Apostles) and the special leadership, or primacy, of the pope (the successor of Saint Peter the Apostle) among the bishops.

The pope as the successor of Saint Peter and head of the College of Bishops has a special authority in the Church. He has "supreme, full, immediate, and universal power in the care of souls." When the pope and the bishops act together in their capacity as the College of Bishops, they exercise supreme and full teaching authority over the universal Church.

Infallibility is the charism of the Holy Spirit given to the Church that guarantees that the official teaching of the pope or the pope and bishops on matters of faith and morals is without error. This charism is at work when:

- the pope teaches officially as the supreme pastor of the Church, or
- the College of Bishops teaches together with the pope.

The Catholic faithful are required to accept such teachings with the "obedience of faith" (Romans 16:26).

FAITH CONNECTION

Develop several interview questions you would like to ask your pastor about the teachings of the Catholic Church. Invite him to discuss the questions with the class.

_____

_____

_____

Parish Councils

All the baptized are called to work together to build up the Church. One way we do this work is through parish councils. A parish council is made up of representatives of the parish family. These representatives are either appointed by the pastor or elected by parishioners and approved by the pastor.

The Work of Parish Councils

Parish councils help the pastor with his managerial and pastoral tasks. They work with him in such areas as finance, justice, education, and service. Parish councils foster a sense of community by developing and promoting programs that touch the lives of the members of the parish. They also help the parish reach out to the members of the wider community. Parish councils are often organized into dynamic committees. Examples of these committees include finance, administration, education, social justice, spiritual development, ecumenism, evangelism, and parish activities.

Sharing Our Gifts

A parish community contains a whole host of people who use their talents and skills to build up the Church and take part in her mission. For example, parishioners who are social workers, artists, nurses, skilled laborers, merchants, business leaders, secretaries, lawyers, doctors, educators, and so on, can use their gifts to help create vibrant faith communities.

Among the issues that councils tackle are the continuing need for parish volunteers, youth education, development and implementation of parish mission statements, caring for the needy, parent education, and the challenges of the fewer number of priests to serve a growing Catholic population.

How does your parish organize itself to touch the lives of both members of the parish and members of the wider community?

WHAT DIFFERENCE

Does Faith Make in My Life?

Belonging to Groups

We all have a basic need to belong. Humans were not made to live in isolation; we need other people. Yes, there are times when we choose to be alone, but we all like to belong to groups where we are accepted, have fun, and work together.

Through Baptism you have the wonderful gift of being joined to Christ and belonging to the Church, the Body of Christ. We all belong to the family of God. We have the responsibility of showing others that we are all God's children.

Throughout your life you will belong to many other groups. Your own families, classes in school, teams, clubs, and organizations are only a few examples. Members of a group share things with others, learn to trust each other, recognize one another's gifts and talents, and learn how to work together.

Sometimes it is a challenge to work with a group. To be a vibrant member of any group you have to learn how to get along, how to play fair, and how to work together for the common good of the group.

Here are some suggestions to help you be a responsible and valued member of any group.

* Value being a member of the group.

* Have a spirit of cooperation and an open mind.

* Be respectful of other members and their ideas.

* Express your opinions honestly, in a give-and-take of ideas.

* Be a part of the planning of projects, the brainstorming of ideas, or the solution of problems.

* Decide who will do what, when tasks will be accomplished.

* Work cooperatively for the good of the group.

* Meet your responsibilities.

* Ask God's blessings on the group.

* Pray for God's help in accomplishing your goals.

Faith Decision

• In your journal or on a piece of paper describe the best group to which you have ever belonged. Using the list on this page describe your experience in that particular group.

• Choose one suggestion from the list that you can work on developing so that you can be a more active member of your parish.

This week I will contribute to the work of my parish by

_____

_____

_____

_____

_____.

PRAY and REVIEW

Prayer of God's People

Leader:
O LORD, happy are those who trust in you.

All:
Happy are those who live in your Temple, singing praise to you.

Group 1:
I long to be in your Temple,

Group 2:
Even sparrows have built nests near your altars.

All:
Happy are those who live in your Temple, singing praise to you.

Group 1:
One day spent in your Temple is better than one thousand spent elsewhere.

Group 2:
I would rather be a doorkeeper at your Temple than live in the homes of the wicked.

All:
Happy are those who live in your Temple, singing praise to you.

Group 1:
The LORD is our protector, blessing us with love and honor.

Group 2:
The LORD does not withhold anything from those who do right.

All:
Happy are those who live in your Temple, singing praise to you.

BASED ON PSALM 84

Leader:
Lord God, you call us
to be your Church.
May we always be aware that we live in your presence, one God who is Father, Son, and Holy Spirit.

All: Amen.

FAITH VOCABULARY

Define each of these terms:

1. Body of Christ
2. Temple of the Holy Spirit
3. charisms
4. Marks of the Church
5. ecumenism
6. apostolic succession
7. Magisterium
8. infallibility

MAIN IDEAS

Choose either (a) or (b) from each set of items. Write a brief paragraph to answer each of your choices.

1. (a) Discuss what it means to say the Church is a mystery.

   (b) Describe how the images Body of Christ and Temple of the Holy Spirit help us understand the mystery of the Church.

2. (a) Explain how the Marks of the Church help us understand the mystery of the Church.

   (b) Explain how the work of the Magisterium helps us live as faithful and responsible members of the Church.

CRITICAL THINKING

Using what you have learned in this chapter, reflect on and explain this statement:
   God invites everyone to salvation.

FAMILY DISCUSSION

How is our family a sign that the Church is the Body of Christ?

For more ideas on ways your family can live your faith, visit the "Faith First for Families" page at **www.FaithFirst.com**. Also click on Teen Center and read this week's interactive story.

Paul the Apostle
A Scripture Story

3

FAITH FOCUS

How did Saint Paul spread the Gospel throughout the Roman Empire?

FAITH VOCABULARY

missionary   Acts of the Apostles

martyr

Think about a trip you took that didn't go as you planned. How did you feel? What did you do?

People often take trips. Trips share one thing in common: We go some place for a reason or purpose. For example, we might visit relatives or go on vacation. Some trips are just what we expected. Other trips are full of surprises, even with unexpected adventures.

The Acts of the Apostles tells about the trips made by Saint Paul the Apostle. His trips were planned, but they were filled with unexpected adventures.

What do you already know about Saint Paul's travels?

Saint Paul the Apostle, mosaic

Paul . . . called to be an apostle and set apart for the gospel of God.
ROMANS 1:1

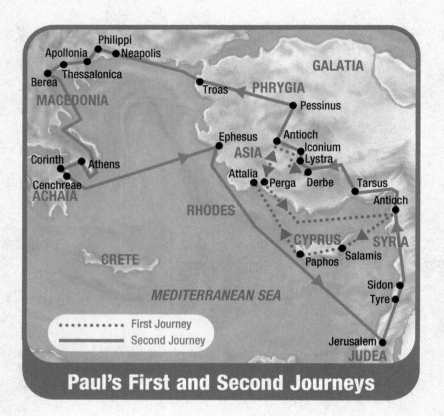

Paul's First and Second Journeys

Key:
- • • • • • • First Journey
- ——— Second Journey

The Missionary Journeys of Saint Paul the Apostle

Before he became known as Paul, his Roman name, he was known by his Jewish name Saul. Saul became Paul the Apostle, the great missionary to the Gentiles, or people who were not Jewish.

A Christian **missionary** is one who carries out Christ's mission to preach the Gospel to all nations. As a missionary, Saint Paul traveled by land and by sea. The **Acts of the Apostles** tells us that Saint Paul made four missionary journeys. The first three took him throughout Syria, Asia Minor, and Macedonia (Greece). His fourth and last journey took him to Rome. There he was put to death because of his faith in Jesus Christ and became a **martyr** of the Church. All his journeys had one purpose: to bring disciples to Jesus.

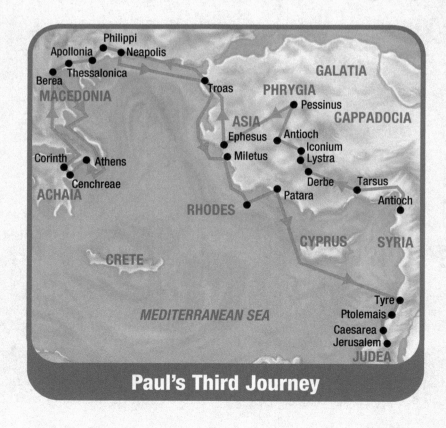

Paul's Third Journey

According to tradition, Saint Paul the Apostle was beheaded on the Ostian Road outside of Rome and was buried in a cemetery nearby. Excavations have verified that there was a pagan cemetery dating from the first and second centuries on this same Ostian Road. In the fourth century, Constantine the Great erected the Basilica of Saint Paul Outside the Walls over the tomb of Saint Paul the Apostle. The current Basilica of Saint Paul Outside the Walls was completed in 1854.

Harbor Scene with Saint Paul's Departure from Caesarea.
Jan Brueghel the Elder (1586–1625), Flemish painter.

Paul's Sea Adventure

On his journey to Rome, Saint Paul was shipwrecked. The story of his shipwreck, which is found in the Acts of the Apostles, follows a popular type of ancient adventure story—the sea voyage. The shipwreck of Paul has all the drama and adventure of one of these tales. It also has one major difference. In these sea voyage adventure stories the hero usually did not stand up to explain the importance of all of his adventures as Saint Paul did.

The hardships and terrors of the sea were proof that there was a divine plan for the journey that Paul was making. God saved Paul from the perils of the sea so that he could continue to ceaselessly spread the Gospel to all people, all the way to Rome. Saint Paul zealously carried out Jesus' command to his disciples to preach the Gospel and "make disciples of all nations" (Matthew 28:19).

Saint Paul's fourth and final journey took him to Rome. He had been in prison in Jerusalem for two years. But as a Roman citizen, Paul was able to appeal his case directly to Caesar and request a trial in Rome. So he set sail for Rome, escorted by a Roman centurion. There he would be put to death for his faith in Christ.

FAITH CONNECTION

Imagine that Saint Paul the Apostle is the patron saint of your parish. Create a motto that both represents him and inspires you to share the Gospel with others.

_____

_____

_____

Paul's Journey to Rome

It was late autumn of A.D. 60 and very close to the time when sea travel stopped because of winter storms. As they traveled on, a storm struck, making it extremely difficult, even for the most skilled hands, to control the ship. Spare cargo and even the ship's tackle were thrown overboard to lighten the ship. The hurricane-force storm blew so fiercely that people started to lose hope.

Detail of Saint Paul preventing soldiers from killing prisoners on board the ship, stained glass

Detail of angel speaking to Saint Paul, stained glass

Paul addressed them:

"I urge you now to keep up your courage; not one of you will be lost, only the ship. For last night an angel of the God to whom [I] belong and whom I serve stood by me and said, 'Do not be afraid, Paul. You are destined to stand before Caesar; and behold, for your sake, God has granted safety to all who are sailing with you.' Therefore, keep up your courage, men; I trust in God that it will turn out as I have been told."

ACTS OF THE APOSTLES 27:22–25

How would you summarize Saint Paul's message of hope in one sentence?

Saint Paul Arriving at Malta.
Peter Mulier (1637–1701),
Dutch painter.

As the storm began to rage and the sea surged, some of the sailors tried to abandon the ship. Again, Saint Paul spoke:

"Today is the fourteenth day that you have been waiting, going hungry and eating nothing. I urge you, therefore, to take some food; it will help you survive. Not a hair of the head of anyone of you will be lost." When he said this, he took bread, gave thanks to God in front of them all, broke it, and began to eat. They were all encouraged, and took some food themselves. In all, there were two hundred seventy-six of us on the ship.   Acts of the Apostles 27:33–37

The ship finally ran aground on a sandbar. But Saint Paul's faith saved everyone.

[T]hey struck a sandbar and ran the ship aground. The bow was wedged in and could not be moved, but the stern began to break up under the pounding [of the waves]. The soldiers planned to kill the prisoners so that none might swim away and escape, but the centurion wanted to save Paul and so kept them from carrying out their plan. He ordered those who could swim to jump overboard first and get to the shore, and then the rest, some on planks, others on debris from the ship. In this way, all reached shore safely.

Acts of the Apostles 27:41–44

Saint Paul the Apostle soon reached safety on the island of Malta. Three months later he again set sail for Rome. When he arrived there, Saint Paul continued to preach Jesus Christ until he was martyred for his faith in Christ.

How does Saint Paul's faith save the people on the shipwrecked boat?

33

Understanding the Word of God

(Top) American teenagers on mission in Peru, playing with children who live in prison with their imprisoned mothers

(Bottom) Missionary from Nigeria distributing Holy Communion to disaster victims in Papua, New Guinea

The Missionary Church

Before the Risen Jesus ascended into heaven, he gave his followers the mission to make disciples of all nations (see Matthew 28:19–20). Spreading the Gospel and making disciples of all nations is exactly what the Apostles did and the Church is called to do. This means that the Church is missionary by nature.

Saint Paul the Apostle's missionary journeys teach us what it means to be a missionary Church.

- Saint Paul showed God's love for everyone when the boat was in danger. This is what the missionary spirit is all about—the energy and vitality of sharing the Gospel of salvation with everyone without exception.
- During the violent storms everyone seemed to totally lose hope. Saint Paul did not.
- The meal that Saint Paul shared with the crew reminded the early Christian readers of the Eucharist. Jesus is present in the Eucharist. He is with us to help us through the rough times.

The Church exists to bring the Good News to every part of the world, so that it may enter the hearts of all people and renew the world. We call this work of the Church evangelization. The Church today brings Christ and the Gospel to all people. We proclaim the Gospel throughout our own countries, and we travel far and wide sharing the Gospel with peoples of all cultures and nations. The Church will continue this mission of announcing the Gospel to all people until the end of time when Christ comes again in glory.

FAITH CONNECTION

How can you live your baptismal calling and responsibility to take part in the missionary work of the Church?

_____

_____

_____

OUR CHURCH
MAKES A DIFFERENCE

Church Youth on Mission

The high school youth group of Saint Mary of the Lake parish in White Bear Lake, Minnesota, participates in the missionary work of the Church in a unique way. Each summer the youth make a journey to a different place in the United States to repair homes for people living in poverty.

One summer the group traveled to Appalachia where families were living in homes that had leaky roofs and broken doors and windows. The repairs to these houses made a big difference in people's lives!

The Catholic community of Saint Gabriel the Archangel in McKinney, Texas, also takes their missionary responsibilities very seriously. The parish sponsors Mission Mexico. Mission Mexico is made up of youth and advisors who travel to Sabinas, Mexico, where they visit Casa Hogar.

Sabinas, Mexico

The youth of both Saint Mary of the Lake and Saint Gabriel's parishes return from their mission trips with a lifetime of memories and a lifetime lesson of spiritual growth. On all their journeys the youth receive much more than they are able to give.

What youth groups do you know about that do missionary work? How can you support or become an active member of one of these mission projects?

Saint Mary of the Lake youth on mission in Appalachia

Saint Gabriel the Archangel youth and adults on mission in Sabinas, Mexico

WHAT DIFFERENCE
Does Faith Make in My Life?

Living with Zeal and Optimism

Optimism

Optimism is an attitude or an emotional inclination or belief that things are good and that all will work out for the best. Christian optimism is based on our belief that God is always there for us. We believe in God who loves us and offers us everlasting life.

Zeal

Saint Paul and those who participate in the missionary work of the Church are filled with zeal. Zeal is eagerness, an intensity of action. Zeal drives someone to act with determination. Every baptized person is called to use their energy, vitality, and zeal to share the teachings of Jesus and the good news of God's love and care for all people.

Optimism is not simply magical thinking. It comes from a trust in God's love and a belief that God wants you to be happy—now and forever in heaven. It is based on your belief that God wants the very best for you and all people. It is a spirit of confidence and cheerfulness that things are going to work out.

What is your attitude toward the way things are going? How do you show that you believe that things are going to work out for the best?

Optimism affects your attitude and your relationship with others. It also affects your mood. Your attitude can either build you up or tear you down.

Zeal and optimism are contagious. As a Christian you are called to be a person of zeal and optimism. When you are worried, or praying for someone, or praying for something to turn out a certain way, you need an optimistic attitude and you need to pray with zeal.

Faith Decision

- How does an optimistic attitude help you live your relationship with God and with others with zeal?

- With a partner decide on one thing you can do together in your school or neighborhood that shows others that you are zealous and optimistic followers of Christ.

Write your plan here.

_____

_____

_____

_____

_____

PRAY and REVIEW

Our Hope Is in the Lord

Leader: The virtue of hope gave Saint Paul the Apostle strength to preach Jesus Christ in times of great adversity and suffering. The Beatitudes proclaimed by Jesus give us the same hope. They give us the vision to see our way through times when it is difficult for us to live our faith in Christ.

Reader: A reading from the holy Gospel according to Matthew.

All: **Glory to you, O Lord.**

Reader: *Proclaim Matthew 5:3–10.* The Gospel of the Lord.

All: **Praise to you, Lord Jesus Christ.**

Group 1: "Blessed are you when they insult you and persecute you and utter every kind of evil against you (falsely) because of me" (Matthew 5:11).

All: **Rejoice in your hope, be patient in tribulation.**

Group 2: "Rejoice and be glad, for your reward will be great in heaven. Thus they persecuted the prophets who were before you" (Matthew 5:12).

All: **Rejoice in your hope, be patient in tribulation.**

Leader: O my God, relying on your infinite goodness and promises we hope to obtain, with the help of your grace and the merits of Jesus Christ, our Lord and Redeemer, life everlasting.

All: **Amen.**

FAITH VOCABULARY

Write a sentence that uses each of these faith terms correctly.

1. missionary
2. Acts of the Apostles
3. martyr

MAIN IDEAS

Choose either (a) or (b) from each set of items. Write a brief paragraph to answer each of your choices.

1. (a) Describe the missionary work of Saint Paul the Apostle.

   (b) Compare Saint Paul's shipwreck with ancient sea voyage stories.

2. (a) Describe the message of hope that Saint Paul brought to the people on the ship during the storm.

   (b) Discuss the statement "The Church is missionary by nature."

CRITICAL THINKING

Using what you have learned in this chapter, reflect on and explain this statement:

Every baptized Christian is charged with the responsibility of being a missionary.

FAMILY DISCUSSION

What can we as a family do to help spread the Gospel to others?

For more ideas on ways your family can live your faith, visit the "Faith First for Families" page at **www.FaithFirst.com**. Also read the Bible story on the Teen Center this week.

The Church: A People of Prayer

4

FAITH FOCUS

How does being a member of the Church help each of us become a person of prayer?

FAITH VOCABULARY

vocal prayer   meditation

contemplation

How is technology changing the way people communicate today?

A major media company named Johannes Gutenberg (1390–1468) as the person of the second millennium. Gutenberg, who invented the technique of printing with movable type, printed the first Bible. Gutenberg's printing techniques revolutionized our ability to communicate with one another.

Prayer is communication—the communication channel linking people and God. Prayer is raising our minds and hearts to God.

What were the first prayers you were taught? What is your favorite way to pray now? How has the Church helped you pray?

It is good to give thanks to the LORD.
PSALM 92:2

In Jesus' Name We Pray

The Praying Church

The Church is a communication community. We are the new People of God. We are joined together as the one Body of Christ, constantly communicating with God through prayer. We raise our voices as one in adoration, blessing, thanksgiving, intercession, petition, and praise of God.

The Holy Spirit, the third Person of the Holy Trinity, continuously invites and teaches the Church to pray.

The Holy Spirit helps us remember the prayer of Abraham and Moses, Ruth and Esther, and the prayer of all the people of the old Covenant. The same Holy Spirit recalls to our memory the prayer of Mary, Peter, and the other disciples. Most of all, the Holy Spirit reminds us of what Jesus said and taught about prayer and forms us into a praying community.

> For those who are led by the Spirit of God are children of God. . . . [Y]ou received a spirit of adoption, through which we cry, "A*bba*, Father!" . . .
>
> In the same way, the Spirit too comes to the aid of our weakness; for we do not know how to pray as we ought, but the Spirit itself intercedes with inexpressible groanings. ROMANS 8:14–15, 26

Describe the Church as a praying community.

The Christian Rhythm of Prayer

The prayer of the Church has a certain rhythm. This rhythm is made up of fixed times and seasons that we can mark off with regularity to ensure that the time we spend in prayer flows throughout our life. These times and seasons include the weekly cycle of prayer centered on the Sunday Eucharist, the cycle of feasts of the Lord and of Mary and of the saints, and the seasons of the liturgical year. There are also daily rhythms to the Church's life of prayer, such as morning and evening prayer, grace before and after meals, and the Liturgy of the Hours.

The simplest, yet very powerful, prayer that we can utter is to speak the name *Jesus* over and over again. This reminds us that every good grace that comes from God the Father comes through Jesus, our Lord and Savior.

Having a regular rhythm to our prayer, like having a regular rhythm to our breathing, reenergizes our spiritual life. Prayer is our encounter with God who is always with us. Prayer strengthens our relationship with the Holy Trinity and with all the members of the Body of Christ. It draws us closer to the love of God. In short, prayer transforms the way we think and act.

Did you Know...

In his youth, Saint Bernard of Clairvaux (1090–1153) enjoyed being alone. When he learned about a newly formed Benedictine monastery, he asked to become a member. Bernard's dedication to the prayer and work of the monastery led others to ask him to found a new monastery that eventually became the center of sixty-eight other monasteries. The work of this quiet, shy boy, which renewed the prayer life of the Church, is still being felt in the Church today. The Church celebrates the feast day of Saint Bernard of Clairvaux, Doctor of the Church, on August 20.

FAITH CONNECTION

Saint Augustine of Hippo once said that the person who sings prays twice. Develop a chant, a rhythmic one-note line of prayer. Write the words here.

_____

_____

_____

Vocal Prayer

Vocal prayer is spoken prayer. It is spoken aloud or spoken within the quiet of our heart. The expression of prayer consists of words that communicate our blessing and adoration, our petition and intercession, our praise and thanksgiving to God.

Meditation

In **meditation** we silently express what is in our heart and on our mind. We use our mind and heart and imagination and our emotions and desires to understand and follow what the Lord is asking of us.

Contemplation

Contemplation is simply being with God. Saint Teresa of Avila (1515–1582), the Spanish mystic and Doctor of the Church, describes contemplative prayer as "nothing else than a close sharing between friends; it means taking time frequently to be alone with him who we know loves us."

How are vocal prayer, meditation, and contemplation similar to one another? How do they differ?

Expressions of Prayer

Think of a time you saw people react to the same situation in different ways. Describe the situation and the ways people expressed themselves.

The truth is that people often express themselves in many different ways. The same is true of our prayer. There are three basic ways Christians express themselves in prayer. These expressions of prayer are vocal prayer, meditation, and contemplation.

Sources of Christian Prayer

The prayer of the Body of Christ, the Church, is nourished and strengthened through Scriptures, through the sacraments and liturgy of the Church, and through the theological virtues of faith, hope, and love. All are God's gifts to us.

Sacred Scripture

Sacred Scripture is the word of God. Through reading and listening to the word of God, we encounter him speaking to us, and we listen to him. We deepen our love for God and respond to that divine love.

Sacraments and Liturgy of the Church

Jesus is present with his Church in the celebration of the sacraments and other liturgical celebrations.

Virtue of Faith

Our prayer, the surge of our heart to God, begins out of faith. We believe God meets us and we meet him in expected and unexpected ways.

Virtue of Hope

Our prayer continues out of hope. We confidently wait, knowing that God listens and responds. He does only what is best for us.

Virtue of Love

Out of love God invites us to share in the communion of the life and love of the Holy Trinity—God the Father, Son, and Holy Spirit. Out of love we respond yes to that divine invitation.

Describe how the sources of Christian prayer can help you grow as a person of prayer.

Faith, Hope, Love, stained glass

All Glory and Honor Is Yours, Almighty Father

Like the prayer of Jesus, the prayer of Christians is addressed primarily to God the Father. We see this in the doxologies that conclude many of the liturgical prayers of the Church. The word *doxology* means "praise-words." For example, at the conclusion of the Eucharistic Prayer we pray:

> Through him [Christ], and with him, and in him, O God, almighty Father, in the unity of the Holy Spirit, all glory and honor is yours, for ever and ever. Amen.
>
> FROM EUCHARISTIC PRAYER, *ROMAN MISSAL*

Christians do not pray only to God the Father. We pray to God the Son, Jesus Christ, and to the Father in Jesus' name. We pray to God the Holy Spirit, our helper and the giver of life, sent to us by the Father and the Son.

However we pray, we can pray anyplace and anytime. The choice of a place to pray is important. While we gather in our parish church for the celebration of the liturgy, the church is also a favorite place for Catholics to come for prayer throughout the day. It is there that Catholics often come to visit with Christ present in the Blessed Sacrament.

Our personal prayer can also be enriched by setting aside a prayer corner in our homes where we can quietly read the Scriptures and listen to God's own word to us. We can also spend time with God during a walk outdoors. No matter where and when we pray, God is always there welcoming us and listening to us.

Prayer and Christian life are inseparable. Filled with the Holy Spirit we join with Jesus Christ, and with Mary and all the saints. Together as the new People of God we offer our lives and raise our voices in praise and thanksgiving to the Father.

FAITH CONNECTION

Design a prayer space for your home. On the lines below, describe the location and what you would include in your prayer space.

_____

_____

_____

_____

_____

Christian Music

From the days of the early Church the followers of Christ have expressed their prayers to God through music (see Ephesians 5:19–20). Through music Christians celebrate and express the depth of their faith in and love for God—in ways they cannot express through words alone.

Psalms

From the days of the Apostles, the followers of Jesus have used music in their prayer life. The Gospel tells us that Jesus and his disciples sang at the Last Supper: "Then, after singing a hymn, they went out to the Mount of Olives" (Matthew 26:30). Singing psalms continues to be an integral part of the worship and prayer life of Christians today.

Hymns

Christians also express their faith through hymns. Some of the hymns that we sing today have lyrics that are based in early Church writings.

Chant

Recently, Gregorian chant has become popular again. This simple yet melodic form of music was developed around the year 900.

Classical Music

It was in the classical period of music, around 1750, that sacred music in the Church in the West reached its height with the Austrian composers Wolfgang Amadeus Mozart (1756–1791) and Franz Joseph Haydn (1732–1809). The Masses and sacred music that they composed blended text, music, and belief in God to a new level.

Organ

Not all the sacred music created by Christian composers was intended to be sung. Many churches, especially the great cathedrals in Europe, had a resident composer as their organist. This person created brilliant new music that was meant to inspire people to lift their minds and hearts to God in silent prayer.

Illustrated manuscript showing Gregorian chant

Music is more than just something in the background to set a mood. Music invites people to participate actively in the liturgy. Music helps us lift our minds and hearts to God in song. Music binds the community together in a communal act of worship.

What is your favorite type of sacred music? How does this music help you express your love for God?

45

WHAT DIFFERENCE

Does Faith Make in My Life?

Meditation

Like the disciples who spent time with Jesus while he was on earth, you too can spend time with Jesus. You can ask him to teach you to pray, to help you understand what it means for you to live as one of his followers. One way you can do this is through the prayer of meditation.

Taking time for meditation is a wonderful gift you can give yourself. Just to take fifteen or twenty minutes away from the noise and busyness of your day can help you relax in body and mind and deepen your relationship with God.

Here are eight steps and some questions to help you get started.

❖ **Set aside some time to meditate.** What time could you set aside? Where would you find your quiet place to pray?
❖ **Quiet your mind and just relax.** What would be the best way for you to do this?
❖ **Pray to the Holy Spirit.** Ask for help to open your mind and listen to God. If you are distracted, just relax and try to refocus your thinking on God's presence.

- ❖ **Choose what you are going to pray about.** It could be a line from a prayer or poem, or a reading from your favorite Scripture story.
- ❖ **Begin your conversation with Jesus.** What do you think Jesus would say to you?
- ❖ **Use your imagination and create a scene.** Picture yourself with Jesus. Where would you be? What would you talk about?
- ❖ **Tell Jesus what's going on in your life right now.** Ask him for what you need. What do you really want Jesus to know about?
- ❖ **Write some thoughts from your meditation in your journal.** Keeping a prayer journal can be helpful in developing a life of prayer.

Faith· Decision

- • Talk to someone you know who uses meditation as a way of praying. Ask this person how meditation helps them.

- • Take some time this week to meditate. Use the eight steps on these pages.

This week I will choose a special time and place to meditate. The time and place I will meditate are:

Time   Place

_____   _____

_____   _____

PRAY and REVIEW

Mary's Prayer of Praise

Leader: Mary is a model of prayer for all Christians. Let us join with Mary in praising God.

All: **"My soul proclaims the greatness of the Lord; my spirit rejoices in God my savior.**

Group 1: For he has looked upon his handmaid's lowliness; behold, from now on will all ages call me blessed.

Group 2: The Mighty One has done great things for me, and holy is his name.

Group 1: His mercy is from age to age to those who fear him.

Group 2: He has shown might with his arm, dispersed the arrogant of mind and heart.

Group 1: He has thrown down the rulers from their thrones but lifted up the lowly.

Group 2: The hungry he has filled with good things; the rich he has sent away empty.

Group 1: He has helped Israel his servant, remembering his mercy,

Group 2: according to his promise to our fathers, to Abraham and to his descendants forever."

All: **"My soul proclaims the greatness of the Lord; my spirit rejoices in God my savior."** LUKE 1:46–55

FAITH VOCABULARY

Define each of these terms:

1. vocal prayer
2. meditation
3. contemplation

MAIN IDEAS

Choose either (a) or (b) from each set of items. Write a brief paragraph to answer each of your choices.

1. (a) Describe the Church as a praying community.

   (b) What do we mean by the rhythm of prayer?

2. (a) Describe vocal prayer, meditation, and contemplation.

   (b) Name and describe the sources of Christian prayer.

CRITICAL THINKING

Using what you have learned in this chapter, reflect on and explain this statement:
Every joy and suffering, every event and need can become the matter of prayer.

FAMILY DISCUSSION

What can we do to strengthen our rhythm of praying together as a family?

For more ideas on ways your family can live your faith, visit the "Faith First for Families" page at **www.FaithFirst.com**. Also check out the extra activity for this chapter on the Teen Center.

The Prayer of the Church

5

FAITH FOCUS

Why is prayer vital to the Christian life?

FAITH VOCABULARY

prayer	Covenant
liturgy	rites
devotions	icons

How do you spend your time at home on a typical day?

Spending time together—that pretty much can summarize many of our days. We move from home to school, to after-school activities, and back into our home again at night.

Prayer is spending time with God, talking and listening to him. Our time with God is so vital that he does not wait for us to come to him. The Holy Spirit tirelessly reaches out to everyone, inviting us to prayer.

When are the best times of day for you to pray?

Service of Light, Easter Vigil

LORD, hear my prayer . . . for to you I entrust my life.
PSALM 143:1, 8

The Call to Prayer

Christian Prayer

Spending time with God—sharing our life with him and listening to him—is at the heart of our relationship with God. The mystery and wonder of **prayer** is that God always begins our conversation with him. God desires that we live in covenant and communion with him.

Prayer as Covenant

The truth is that we are so connected with God that life without him is not possible. God has created us and entered into the **Covenant** with us. He is with us in every moment of our lives. Through Baptism we are joined to Christ, the new and everlasting Covenant. We are united in Christ with the Father and the Holy Spirit. Christian prayer is an expression of that covenantal relationship with God.

Prayer as Communion

Our prayer is a sign that our life as children of God is alive. In Baptism we are united with Christ. When we pray, we are living, in a very important way, our relationship, or communion, with God the Father,

with his Son, Jesus Christ, and with the Holy Spirit (see Ephesians 3:18–21).

Obstacles of Prayer

The truth is that communicating with God on a regular basis each day just takes practice and hard work. Why do we struggle with prayer? There are many reasons. Some of them are:

- We misunderstand what prayer really is.
- We become discouraged when we pray and do not see results.
- We are sometimes so busy and distracted that God cannot get a word in.

Prayer has the power to help us see God in the people around us and in the ordinary events of our daily lives. It has the power to help us remember that we are children of God with whom he shares his life and love.

What other things can be obstacles to prayer, to living in covenant and communion with God?

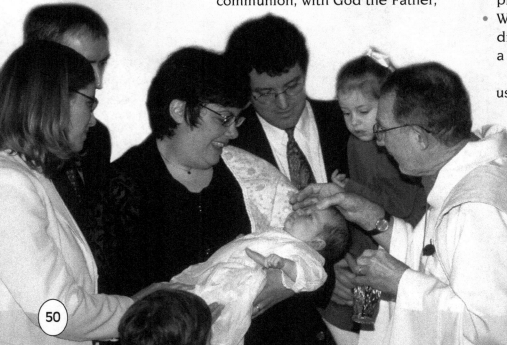

Models of Prayer

In the Scriptures we read about people of prayer. We listen to stories of the many conversations between God and his people. We learn how they prayed and overcame the obstacles to their prayer.

Abraham

We call Abraham our "father in faith" (Eucharistic Prayer I) for good reason. Solely on God's promise to them, Abraham and Sarah and their family packed up all their belongings. In faith they did what God asked. (See Genesis 12:4.)

Moses

From that first moment of his approaching the burning bush, Moses went back and forth in conversation with God. Those face-to-face meetings with God, or moments of contemplative prayer, transformed Moses' life. (See Exodus 33:11.)

David

David, the shepherd-king of God's people, drew up plans to build a temple in which the people would gather in prayer in the presence of God. (See 2 Samuel 7:18–29.)

The Prophets

The Scriptures are also filled with many conversations that Isaiah, Ezekiel, Jeremiah, and other prophets had with God— conversations that refocused the attention of God's people on God and living the Covenant with him and waiting and preparing for the promised Savior. (See Isaiah 6:5, 8, 11; Jeremiah 20:7–18.)

Mary

The Blessed Virgin Mary is a model of prayer for Christians. By reflecting on her life, we learn how vocal prayer, meditation, and contemplation all help us express our prayer to God.

Trusting in God's promises to his people, Mary unexpectedly learned that God had chosen her to become the mother of his Son, whom she was to name Jesus. "Behold, I am the handmaid of the Lord. May it be done to me according to your word" was Mary's response (Luke 1:38).

Mary was a woman of prayer. Mary lived a life of faith, hope, and love. God's love for her and her love for God filled her heart in a way that no one before had ever experienced. Mary's heart was in rhythm with the heart of God, and she said, "Yes."

Madonna and child, Native American painting. Artist unknown.

FAITH CONNECTION

Look up and read the Scripture passages on this page. Name who each Scripture passage tells about. Describe how that person is a model of prayer for Christians.

Person	Description
_____	_____
_____	_____
_____	_____
_____	_____
_____	_____

Jesus praying, bronze sculpture in Garden of Gethsemane overlooking Jerusalem

night. Going off to be alone in prayer, Jesus turned to his Father and spoke of his fears and his trust:

"My Father, if it is possible, let this cup pass from me; yet, not as I will, but as you will."

MATTHEW 26:39

Jesus' whole life was a life of prayer. He lived his life on earth in continuing conversation with his Father. Jesus acknowledged his Father as God. He blessed and thanked his Father as the source of all blessings. He prayed for himself and for others, always confident in his Father's love for him, for his disciples, and for all people.

Describe how the prayer of Jesus teaches us to pray.

The Prayer of Jesus

Jesus most fully reveals the way of prayer. Jesus taught us to pray, "Our Father in heaven." He invited us to approach God the Father in prayer and trust him as "Abba," a loving Father whose most driving concern in life was the good and well-being of his children.

Throughout his life on earth, Jesus did just that. Time and time again Jesus spent time alone with his Father before making important decisions. During these conversations with his Father he came to see more clearly the work his Father sent him to do. In prayer Jesus received the courage and wisdom to do that work.

To prepare for his imminent suffering and death, Jesus invited his disciples to join with him in prayer outdoors in the quiet of the

The Prayer of the Church

The whole life of the Body of Christ, the Church, is a life of prayer as the life of Jesus was. Saint Paul the Apostle reminds us of how vital prayer is for our life. He writes:

Pray without ceasing. In all circumstances give thanks, for this is the will of God for you in Christ Jesus.

1 THESSALONIANS 5:17–18

Christian prayer rises out of faith, out of hope, and out of love for God. Our prayer ascends in the Holy Spirit through Christ to the Father. God's blessing in turn descends upon us through Christ in the Holy Spirit, showering upon us his many gifts.

Why do we say that the life of a Christian is a life of prayer?

The Liturgy of the Church

The center of the prayer life of the Church is the **liturgy**, especially the celebration of the Eucharist. The liturgy of the Church is the worship of God. It is the work of the whole Christ, Head and Body.

Joined to Christ we give praise and thanksgiving to God the Father through the power of the Holy Spirit. We adore God the Father as the source of all the blessings of creation and salvation he has given us through his Son. We bless him for the gift of the Spirit through whose power we are able to call God Abba, or Father.

Liturgical Rites

For nearly two thousand years, the Church has developed a rich diversity of ways, or **rites**, of celebrating the liturgy. The largest number of Catholics belong to the Roman rite. In addition to the Roman rite, there are other rites that are celebrated by Catholics around the world. Among these are the Byzantine, Alexandrian (or Coptic), and Chaldean rites.

Multiethnic People Encircled by Hands. José Ortega (1921–), Spanish painter.

Local Customs

Like diversity throughout our nation, diversity in the Catholic Church is a source of enrichment. Properly recognized diversity in the celebration of the liturgy reveals the catholicity, or universality, of the Church.

How does the Church go about showing we are one Church made up of many diverse liturgical traditions? We need to follow the guidelines that the local ordinary, the bishop of our diocese or the archbishop of our archdiocese, establishes. While the bishop has many other responsibilities, he is the primary liturgist in any local, or particular, church.

Singing and Music

The music we use in our worship celebrations should reflect the cultural genius and roots of the people gathered to praise and bless God. This does not mean that any type of music—for example, the music and lyrics of the latest pop hit—can be inserted into the celebration of the liturgy. The music needs to be in conformity with the Church's norms.

When we take part in the celebration of any liturgical celebration during which the music mixes with the other sacred rites, something deep inside of us is moved. Something deeply spiritual stirs within our hearts and minds. Our emotions are engaged. Our hearts and heads together seem to be in touch with God.

Explain how the diversity of the Church is shown in the liturgy of the Church.

The Church responds to the Spirit's call to prayer all throughout the day. The Church does this by praying the Liturgy of the Hours. The Liturgy of the Hours, also known as the Divine Office, is the public daily prayer of the Church. The two most important parts are Morning Prayer, also called Lauds, and Evening Prayer, also called Vespers. The other prayers that make up the Liturgy of the Hours are the Office of Readings, Daytime Prayer, and Night Prayer.

Popular Devotions

In addition to the liturgy, our Christian life is nourished by a wide variety of popular **devotions** and piety. Popular devotions are acts of personal or communal prayer. These devotions surround and arise out of the celebration of the liturgy. They enrich and help us express and celebrate the mystery of our life in Christ.

You could spend a very rewarding lifetime traveling the world and witnessing the vastness and diversity of ways Christians celebrate their faith. All these expressions of popular piety and devotion help Christians extend the meaning of the liturgy into their homes and daily living.

Sacred Images

For centuries the Church has used sacred images, such as statues and **icons**. An icon is a picture or image of Christ, Mary, a saint, or an angel. All sacred images used in liturgical celebrations are related to Christ. When we

Our Lady of Guadalupe, mural on building, San Francisco, California

venerate and admire Mary and the angels and the saints, we do so because each of them manifests some aspect of Christ and his work of salvation.

Christian images and other works of art enable the people and events of salvation history to become part of all cultures. They help Christians around the world remember and share in the events of Jesus' life, Passion, death, Resurrection, and Ascension.

Mary and Jesus, mosaic

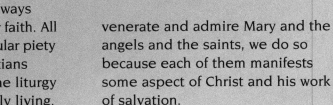

FAITH CONNECTION

Name your favorite popular devotion or sacred work of art. Describe how it enriches your life of faith in Christ.

_____

_____

_____

OUR CHURCH
MAKES A DIFFERENCE

Forms of Spirituality

The Holy Spirit invites and teaches us to pray. He silently awaits us to join in that conversation. Living our life in response to the Holy Spirit is called spirituality.

The history of Christian spirituality reveals how numerous groups in the Church throughout the world came to live the life of Christ authentically and integrally. There is no one way of living our life in Christ. Here is an overview of three of the many paths, or forms, of Christian spirituality.

Monastic Spirituality

Monastic spirituality is a form of religious life in which men and women take vows or promises of poverty, chastity, and obedience. These individuals separate themselves from society either singly (as hermits) or in communities known as monasteries, abbeys, or priories. The goal of monasticism is to pursue, under the guidance of a common rule (such as the Rule of Saint Benedict), a life devoted to prayer and work for the glory of God and the good of the Church and the world.

Franciscan Spirituality

The spirituality of the followers of Saint Francis of Assisi (ca. 1181–1226) puts its emphasis on imitating the total obedience and self-giving of Jesus to his Father. Followers of Saint Francis choose, as Francis did, to live their lives in a way that emphasizes their total dependence on God.

Lay Spirituality

Lay spirituality addresses the daily challenges of men and women who live their lives in Christ in the midst of the world. It keeps living one's relationship with God at the heart of raising families, attending school, or pursuing careers.

What elements in these three forms of spirituality would you like to emphasize in living your life in Christ?

Junior high teacher helping students

Monks at prayer

Franciscan Poor Clare sister making vestments

WHAT DIFFERENCE
Does Faith Make in My Life?

Journal Writing

There are different schools of spirituality and there are different ways to pray. Journal writing is a way of praying that helps you discover God's daily working in your life. Keeping a journal helps you express any special feelings you have, or describe special events of each day where you feel God's presence in your life. A spiritual journal is different from a diary—yet there are similarities. You usually write very personal things in your diary, such as thoughts, feelings, fears, and joys. The wonderful thing about keeping a spiritual journal is that you are sharing all those very special thoughts, feelings, fears, and joys with God.

Your spiritual journal is your dialogue with God, your personal prayer. You can write words, sentences, thoughts, or feelings. You can scribble, write fast, and not worry about grammar or misspelled words, remembering that God knows what's in your heart and what you want to share with him before you write it.

You can also write quotes, good ideas, and thoughts from reading Scripture. You can write lines of a poem you heard or read, and, of course, you can create your own poems, prayers, or songs. You can draw pictures; you can paste in pictures or newspaper clippings—anything you want to remember and share with God that day. It can help you gain a new awareness of God revealing himself in your life.

SEPTEMBER 26

Today was a great day.
Nanna came to visit. The
first time in six years.
Lauren and Chelsea came
over to visit. Nanna had
everyone laughing. She still
is the best storyteller ever!
As Lauren and Chelsea were
leaving, they said, "Now we
know where you get your smile!"
Thanks God!

Here are a few basic steps to get you started.

❖ **Find the right book** (a book of blank pages or a notebook) **or paper** (loose leaf or legal pads) and the pen or pencil you want to use. Keep these in one special place.

❖ **Decide how often you will write** in your journal. If daily, you can establish a routine, a daily form of prayer.

❖ **Find a time and a place to write.** Choose a place free of noise and interruption.

❖ **Relax and pray to the Holy Spirit.** Ask the Holy Spirit to enlighten your mind and open your heart.

❖ **Date each entry.** This will help you go back and find it easily.

❖ **Just begin to write.** Write quickly and don't worry about punctuation or spelling. Be aware of your inner thoughts, feelings, beliefs, and any new insights you discover.

❖ **Write anything that comes to your mind.** Use your writing as your personal dialogue with God, and listen to his response in your heart.

Faith Decision

• How can journal writing help you learn more about yourself and deepen your faith in God?

_____

_____

_____

_____

• What are the best day, time, and place for you to write in your journal?

Day _____

Time _____

Place _____

This week I will begin my journal on

_____ .

PRAY and REVIEW

Prayer Before a Crucifix

Leader: Let us listen to Jesus' prayer to his Father, which he prayed aloud from the cross.

Reader 1: *Proclaim Luke 23:32–34.*

Reader 2: *Proclaim Luke 23:44–49.*

Leader: The crucifix is a sacred image that reminds us of the infinite love of Christ. Spend a few minutes in silent prayer before the crucifix. Conclude by quietly praying this prayer.

All: Good and gentle Jesus,
I see and ponder your five
  wounds.
My eyes behold what King
  David
prophesied about you:
"They have pierced my
  hands and feet;
they have counted all my
  bones."
Engrave on me the image of
  yourself.
Fulfill the yearnings of my
  heart:
give me faith, hope, and love,
true sorrow for my sins,
and true conversion of life.
  Amen.

FAITH VOCABULARY

Define each of these faith terms:

1. prayer
2. Covenant
3. liturgy
4. rites
5. devotions
6. icons

MAIN IDEAS

Choose either (a) or (b) from each set of items. Write a brief paragraph to answer each of your choices.

1. (a) Describe prayer as covenant and as communion with God.

   (b) Describe the prayer of Jesus.

2. (a) What is the role of the liturgy in the prayer life of the Church?

   (b) Describe how popular devotions and sacred images enrich the prayer life of Catholics.

CRITICAL THINKING

Using what you have learned in this chapter, reflect on and explain this statement:
Prayer is a surge of the heart toward God.
SAINT THÉRÈSE OF LISIEUX

FAMILY DISCUSSION

How does family prayer strengthen our relationships with one another?

For more ideas on ways your family can live your faith, visit the "Faith First for Families" page at **www.FaithFirst.com.** Check out "Family Prayer" and include the prayer in your family's prayer time this week.

UNIT ONE

A. The Best Response

Read each statement and circle the best answer.

1. Which of the following is a teaching of Saint Paul about the Church?
   - A. Exodus
   - B. Body of Christ
   - C. Bread of Life
   - D. New Jerusalem

2. What do we call the people of the Church who are not ordained or consecrated religious?
   - A. laypeople
   - B. missionaries
   - C. clergy
   - D. deacons

3. What are the four Marks of the Church?
   - A. one, holy, faithful, catholic
   - B. one, holy, moral, faithful
   - C. one, holy, catholic, apostolic
   - D. holy, apostolic, faithful, catholic

4. What is the term the Church uses to name the connection of all popes and bishops back to Saint Peter and the other Apostles?
   - A. apostolic succession
   - B. Gospel connection
   - C. Sacred Tradition
   - D. deposit of faith

5. What is the vocation of all Christians?
   - A. to share in the work of the Church
   - B. to share in the Paschal Mystery of Christ
   - C. to be happy with God forever
   - D. all of the above

B. Matching Words and Phrases

Match the faith terms in column A with the descriptions in column B.

Column A

____ 1. meditation

____ 2. infallibility

____ 3. contemplation

____ 4. devotions

____ 5. Magisterium

____ 6. vocal prayer

____ 7. doxologies

____ 8. Temple of the Holy Spirit

____ 9. liturgy

____ 10. ecumenism

Column B

a. the indwelling of the Holy Spirit in the Church

b. the teaching authority of the Church

c. prayer and work for the restoration of the unity of the Church

d. acts of individual or communal prayer that rise out of liturgy

e. the charism that guarantees that the official teaching of the pope or the pope and bishops on matters of faith and morals is without error

f. the work and worship of the whole people of God

g. prayer spoken out loud or in the quiet of one's heart

h. using one's mind, heart, imagination, and emotions to express the desire to follow Christ

i. praise words that conclude many liturgical prayers of the Church

j. taking time to be alone with God

C. What I Have Learned

Using what you learned in Unit One, write a reflection about each of the following statements.

1. The Communion of Saints is a communion of holy things and of holy people.

_____

_____

2. There are many models of prayer found in Sacred Scripture.

_____

_____

D. From a Scripture Story

On a separate sheet of paper do the following.

Recall the missionary zeal of Saint Paul the Apostle. Through faith and love, Saint Paul gave the people on the shipwrecked boat a sense of hope. Write a message of your own about how sharing your faith in Christ can be a source of hope for people.

UNIT TWO
Worship and Sacraments

How does the Church celebrate the presence of the Risen Lord in our midst?

Getting Ready

Liturgy and the Sacraments

What do you already know about the signs and symbolic actions of the sacraments?

Sacraments of Christian Initiation

_____

_____

Sacraments of Healing

_____

_____

Sacraments at the Service of Communion

_____

_____

Faith Vocabulary

Put an X next to the faith vocabulary terms that you know. Put a ? next to the faith vocabulary terms that you need to know more about.

_____ Paschal Mystery

_____ liturgical year

_____ sacraments

_____ Baptism

_____ Confirmation

_____ Eucharist

_____ Blessed Sacrament

_____ Reconciliation

_____ Anointing of the Sick

_____ Holy Orders

_____ Matrimony

Questions I Have

What questions about the sacraments and the worship of the Church do you hope these chapters will answer?

_____

_____

_____

_____

A Scripture Story

Jesus and Nicodemus

What do you know about the Gospel account of Jesus meeting with Nicodemus?

Give Thanks to the Lord

The Seven Sacraments,
stained glass

FAITH FOCUS

What does the Church do when we celebrate the liturgy?

FAITH VOCABULARY

sacraments

Paschal Mystery

grace

liturgical year

Think about the people, events, and places on which you focus.

In the movie *Star Wars: The Phantom Menace*, young Anakin Skywalker is told, "Focus determines reality." Skywalker was being taught one of life's important lessons: Those things to which we devote time and on which we focus our attention have a major influence on who we are.

God is the focus, or center, of our lives. We celebrate and remind ourselves of this basic truth when we celebrate the liturgy.

How does the liturgy help you keep God at the center of your life?

Your word is a lamp for my feet, / a light for my path.
PSALM 119:105

Sharing in God's Saving Love

The Worship of the Father

Jesus focused his life on earth on the Father. Joined to Christ at Baptism, we focus all of our attention on God. When we gather together as the new People of God at the liturgy, we join with Jesus, the Head of his Body, the Church. Through the power of the Holy Spirit we give thanks and praise to God the Father as the source of all the blessings of creation and salvation.

By spending time with the Father and focusing on his love, we share more fully in the life of God, and we welcome him into our lives. We see and appreciate that from the beginning of time God has always done and will continue to do what is good for us.

Why do many people say they feel closer to God at Mass than at other times?

With the Son

Through the work of the liturgy, Christ's work of salvation is made present and carried out among us. Christ is always present and leads his Church in the celebration of the liturgy.

- Christ is present in the priest, who acts in the Person of Christ.
- Christ is present in the assembly.
- Christ is present in the living word of God, the Scriptures.
- Christ is present, most importantly, in the Eucharist under the appearances of bread and wine.

It is always "through him, and with him, and in him, . . . in the unity of the Holy Spirit" (Doxology, Eucharistic Prayer) that we give praise and thanks to the Father.

Describe why the liturgy of the Church is the work of the whole Church, Christ the Head and his Body.

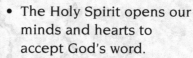

The work of God among us is called the mission of God. We speak of creation as the work of the Father, salvation as the work of the Son, and sanctification as the work of the Holy Spirit. The truth is that while each of these works is attributed to one of the three divine Persons of the Trinity, all these works are the work of all three Persons of the Trinity.

- The Holy Spirit opens our minds and hearts to accept God's word.
- The Holy Spirit makes the saving work of Christ present and real to us by his transforming power.
- The Holy Spirit, especially through the Eucharist, brings us into communion with Christ and one another.

The ultimate work of the Holy Spirit is to draw us more deeply both into the mystery and reality of the Holy Trinity and into loving relationship with one another.

Holy Spirit, stained glass

Through the Power of the Holy Spirit

The mission, or work, attributed to the Holy Spirit is to make us sharers in God's life. In the liturgy the Holy Spirit does this in four ways.

- The Holy Spirit prepares us to meet Christ and join with him. The Holy Spirit prepares our hearts to accept God's gift of himself and to share in God's saving plan of salvation.

FAITH CONNECTION

Write a verse that gives thanks to God the Father, Son, and Holy Spirit.

_____

_____

The Sacraments

The **sacraments** make us sharers in the **Paschal Mystery.** The Paschal Mystery is the saving events of the Passion, death, Resurrection, and glorious Ascension of Jesus Christ. Through this mystery we have been drawn into and made sharers in the mystery of the divine life of the Holy Trinity.

The celebration of Christ's Paschal Mystery in the liturgy and sacraments is unique. The sacraments are effective signs instituted by Christ and entrusted to the Church, by which **grace,** or the divine life of God, is shared with us. Through our taking part in the celebration of the sacraments, our life is changed, or transformed, and we become sharers in the life of God. The Church celebrates seven sacraments, which are classified into three groups:

- Sacraments of Christian Initiation: Baptism, Confirmation, and Eucharist
- Sacraments of Healing: Penance and Reconciliation, or Reconciliation, and Anointing of the Sick
- Sacraments at the Service of Communion: Holy Orders and Matrimony

The three sacraments of Baptism, Confirmation, and Holy Orders each imprint on the person who receives these sacraments an indelible, or permanent, character that remains forever. This is the reason a person can receive these sacraments only one time.

Describe why taking part in the celebration of the sacraments changes your life.

BAPTISM

CONFIRMATION

EUCHARIST

PENANCE AND RECONCILIATION

Common Elements

There are certain common characteristics, or elements, that all the sacraments share. These characteristics help us understand why the sacraments are necessary for the salvation of believers.

- Christ is the principal celebrant of every sacrament.
- The sacraments are effective signs of grace. This means that each sacrament actually accomplishes what it signifies. This happens even if the human minister of the sacrament is unworthy.
- All sacraments are instituted, or given to us, by Christ.
- The celebration of the sacraments is both the work of Christ and the work of the Church. The ordained minister of the Church—bishop, priest, or deacon—leads the celebration of the sacraments. Ordained to serve the Church, he acts in the name and Person of Christ.
- The sacraments are sensible signs of the Holy Spirit's work.

Rites of the Sacraments

Each of the sacraments has a rite approved by the Church for its celebration. A rite is the way something is regularly done. The words and actions the Church uses to celebrate the sacraments are called the rites of the sacraments. The rite used for the celebration of each sacrament has many parts. Some of these parts are divinely given and are unchangeable. For example, a person being baptized is always immersed in water or water is poured over the person's head as the priest or deacon says the words, "(Name), I baptize you in the name of the Father, and of the Son, and of the Holy Spirit" (Rite of Baptism).

The rite of a sacrament also has parts that the Church can adapt and change. For example, before Vatican Council II (1962–1965), Latin, the official language of the Church, was the most widely used language in the celebration of the liturgy by the Roman Catholic Church. Today Mass is celebrated in each country around the world using the vernacular, or the common language used by the people.

Describe the rites of the Mass. What things are the same each week? What things differ from Sunday to Sunday?

The Liturgical Year

As we gather for Eucharist each Sunday we notice that throughout the year the color of the priest's and deacon's vestments changes. We may see green, white, purple (or violet), or red. Hymns and readings change too. All these changing elements help us recognize the feast or season of the **liturgical year** we are celebrating. The liturgical year is the cycle of seasons and feasts the Church celebrates each year.

Sunday. Sunday is the weekly celebration of the Resurrection. It is the Lord's Day. From the days of the early Church, Sunday has been ranked as the first holy day of all.

Advent and Christmas. During the liturgical seasons of Advent and Christmas, we prepare for and celebrate the Incarnation and Nativity and the announcement of Jesus as the Savior of the world.

Lent, Easter Triduum, and Easter. During Lent catechumens prepare for their initiation into the Church. All the faithful join with them and renew their own Baptism. The whole Church prepares for the celebration of Christ's Passion, death, and Resurrection. Holy Thursday, Good Friday, and the celebration of Easter Vigil/Easter Sunday are the most important days of the liturgical year. We call these days—which begin with the celebration of the evening Mass of the Lord's Supper and conclude with Vespers on Easter Sunday—the Easter Triduum, or simply the Triduum, a term which means three days.

Ordinary Time. The longest part of the liturgical year is called Ordinary Time. The word *ordinary* comes from a Latin word meaning "number." On these numbered weeks of the year—for example, the Thirteenth Sunday in Ordinary Time—we listen to the events of the public ministry of Jesus and respond to his invitation to live as his disciples.

Solemnities, Feasts, and Memorials. The Church also celebrates a yearly cycle of feasts. These include the holy days of obligation and other days, such as the solemnity of Christ the King, and days remembering Mary, the Apostles, and the other saints.

FAITH CONNECTION

Plan the design of a new banner for your classroom prayer space to celebrate an upcoming liturgical season or feast. In this space write the words you would use on the banner.

_____

_____

OUR CHURCH
MAKES A DIFFERENCE

Sacramentals

In addition to the seven sacraments the Church celebrates sacramentals. Sacramentals are sacred signs instituted by the Church. The sacramentals prepare us to participate in the sacraments and make us aware of and responsive to God's loving presence in our lives.

Sacramentals include objects, such as the altar, the crucifix, the rosary, and statues. They also include blessings, which are the most important sacramentals of the Church. Among the sacramentals, the blessing of people, meals, objects, and places comes first. Every blessing praises God for his gifts and asks that we use these gifts according to the spirit of the Gospel.

The Blessing of Newly Professed Religious

Some members of the Church are consecrated, or professed, religious. Moved by the Holy Spirit, they promise or vow to live the Gospel with all their heart, joined with others in a religious community. During the ceremony in which religious consecrate their lives to God, they receive a special blessing of the Church.

With the grace of the Holy Spirit, some religious resolve to spend their whole life in the generous service of God's people. Others resolve to live for God alone, in solitude and silence, persevering in prayer and penance, in humble work and holiness of life.

In what ways are professed religious reminders to all the baptized to live the Great Commandment (see Matthew 22:34–40)?

Blessing of a religious sister during Rite of Religious Profession

Blessing of shrimp fleet, Delcambre Shrimp Festival, Delcambre, Louisiana

Blessing of dogs outside Church of Saint Francis, Lima, Peru

WHAT DIFFERENCE

Does Faith Make in My Life?

Recognizing God's Presence

The Catholic Church—through the liturgy, the sacraments, and sacramentals—makes us aware of and encourages us to respond to the constant, loving presence of God in our daily lives.

One of the wonderful truths of our faith is that God is always present with us. He is not only in heaven but right here within each person.

There are times when you may be very aware of the closeness of God. Then there are times when you just get so wrapped up in what's going on that you totally forget that God is right here—right now. How can you develop the daily habit of recognizing God, thanking him, and praising him for his loving presence?

Here are a few steps to develop an awareness of God's presence.

❖ Become more conscious of your surroundings. Look for the beauty in God's creation.
—a smile on someone's face
—a cloud-filled sky
—a playful pet
—a friend's laugh
Say a conscious, deliberate thank-you to God for each of these wonders of creation.

❖ Take time to appreciate the gifts God has given you.
—your very life
—your family and friends
—your gifts and talents
—each new day
Think of ways to show God your appreciation for each of these gracious gifts.

❖ Remember in times of trouble that God is with you.
—when you are separated from someone you love
—when you fail at something important to you
—when nothing seems to be going right
—when an act of violence reminds you of the evil in the world
Ask God to give you the courage, strength, and comfort you need.

As you encounter people try to remind yourself that each person is a child of God.
—family members and friends
—neighbors and classmates
—strangers and those in need
—babies and senior citizens
Thank God for the people in your life and ask God to bless them.

Faith • Decision

- In a small group discuss each of the steps to develop an awareness of God's presence. Add your own examples to each list.

- Make a symbol to remind you that God is always with you. Put it someplace where you will see it each day.

This week I will make a deliberate choice to be aware of God's presence each day by

_____

_____

_____

_____

_____.

PRAY and REVIEW

You Alone Are God!

Group 1:
You are God: we praise you;
you are God:
    we acclaim you;
you are the eternal Father:
    all creation worships you.

Group 2:
To all you angels, all the
    powers of heaven,
cherubim and seraphim,
    sing in endless praise:

All:
**Holy, Holy, Holy Lord
    God of hosts.
Heaven and earth are
    full of your glory.**

Group 1:
Day by day we bless you.
We praise your name for ever.

Group 2:
Keep us today, Lord, from all sin.
Have mercy on us,
    Lord, have mercy.

All:
**Lord, show us your love
    and mercy;
for we put our trust in you.
In you, Lord, is our hope:
and we shall never hope
    in vain. Amen.**

BASED ON THE TE DEUM AND THE HOLY, HOLY, HOLY
FROM THE EUCHARISTIC PRAYER, ROMAN MISSAL

FAITH VOCABULARY

Define each of these terms:

1. sacraments
2. Paschal Mystery
3. grace
4. liturgical year

MAIN IDEAS

Choose either (a) or (b) from each set of items.
Write a brief paragraph to answer each of
your choices.

1. (a) Explain the work of the Trinity in the
       Church's liturgy.

   (b) Describe five ways Christ is present in
       the liturgy.

2. (a) Explain why we say the Church's
       celebration of the liturgy is much more
       than a reenactment of Christ's death,
       Resurrection, and Ascension.

   (b) Describe five elements common to all
       the sacraments.

CRITICAL THINKING

Using what you have learned in this chapter,
reflect on and explain this statement:
    The sacraments are the "masterwork of God"
    celebrating the new and everlasting
    Covenant.

FAMILY DISCUSSION

How does taking part in the liturgy help us
keep God at the center of our family?

For more ideas on ways
your family can live your
faith, visit the "Faith First
for Families" page at
www.FaithFirst.com. Also
click on the Teen Center to
check out the latest games.

Reborn of the Spirit

A Scripture Story

Jesus and Nicodemus,
stained glass

FAITH **FOCUS**

How does the faith story of
Nicodemus help us understand our
own coming to faith in Jesus Christ?

FAITH **VOCABULARY**

Sanhedrin	Pharisee
Torah	eternal life

*Who is in your group of friends? With
whom do you choose to spend time?*

Often we choose as our friends
people who are a lot like us. Jesus
revealed God's love to everyone
without exception. Look at the
group of Jesus' closest disciples.
They were made up of fishermen,
laborers, politicians, zealot party
members, and even a tax
collector.

*What does the Gospel tell us about the
people whom Jesus chose to be his
friends and disciples?*

"Do not be amazed that I told you, 'You must be born from above.'"

JOHN 3:7

Pharisees Question Jesus.
James J. Tissot (1836–1902),
French painter.

Nicodemus

The Gospel names many of the friends and disciples of Jesus. Among those mentioned by Saint John the Evangelist is Nicodemus. We first meet Nicodemus in the third chapter of the Gospel according to John, where he secretly met Jesus in the darkness of night. Nicodemus reappears in the seventh chapter of John's Gospel, where he boldly defended Jesus (see John 7:51), and his words earned Nicodemus the disdain of some Jewish leaders. Finally, Nicodemus joined with Joseph of Arimathea to request Jesus' body from Pilate and to bury Jesus according to Jewish law (see John 19:39–42).

Sanhedrin

Nicodemus was a member of the **Sanhedrin.** The Sanhedrin was the supreme governing council of the Jewish people. Its seventy members had jurisdiction over both the religious and the secular laws of the Jewish nation. At one time the Sanhedrin's power included the power to decide on the life or death of Jews brought before it. The high priest was the presiding officer of the Sanhedrin.

Pharisees

Nicodemus was a **Pharisee.** The Pharisees were a lay sect within Judaism whose members dedicated their lives to the strict keeping of the Law found in the **Torah.** The Torah was the Law of God revealed to Moses, which is found in the first five books of the Old Testament.

At the time of Jesus there were only six thousand Pharisees. The name P*harisee*, which means "the separated one," helps us understand how zealous the Pharisees were in dedicating their lives to living the Torah—they separated themselves from ordinary life in order to keep every detail of the Law.

Jesus' Conversation with Nicodemus

The first time we meet Nicodemus he and Jesus were having a long conversation, or discourse. This conversation, which is found in the third chapter of John's Gospel, follows a common writing technique that would have been recognized by John's readers.

- First, the conversation began with Jesus speaking to Nicodemus.
- Second, Nicodemus took the words of Jesus literally and misunderstood Jesus' message, or teaching.
- Third, Jesus explained the real meaning of his message in detail. Jesus' explanation took Nicodemus beyond the literal meaning of Jesus' words.
- Fourth, John the Evangelist reflects on Jesus' explanation.

This pattern would have signaled John's readers to look closely at the give-and-take between Jesus and Nicodemus. They would especially look at Jesus' closing discourse, which contains the explanation of the statements that Nicodemus first interpreted literally.

We know that Nicodemus came to believe in Jesus. Like so many of those who came to believe in Jesus, Nicodemus was an attentive listener who was led by the Holy Spirit.

Did you Know...

The conversation between Jesus and the Samaritan woman at Jacob's well is another well-known Gospel story. This story is the Gospel reading for the Third Sunday of Lent. You can read the conversation between Jesus and the Samaritan woman in John 4:4–42.

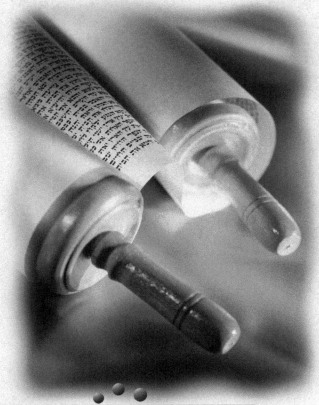

Torah scroll

FAITH ⁙ CONNECTION

Think of one of your favorite Bible stories. Discuss with a partner how your understanding of this story has deepened since you first heard it.

_____

_____

_____

Interview Between Jesus and Nicodemus. James J. Tissot (1836–1902), French painter.

Jesus and Nicodemus

The Gospel account of the conversation between Jesus and Nicodemus is the first of the discourses in the Gospel according to John. This discourse begins with a dialogue between Jesus and Nicodemus (see John 3:1–10). It then shifts to a monologue by Jesus (see John 3:11–15). A monologue is a long speech delivered by a character in a story or poem or by an actor on a stage. Finally, the passage concludes with a reflection by John the Evangelist on the meaning of Jesus' message, or teaching (see John 3:16–21).

Dialogue

Nicodemus was curious when he came to Jesus. He was also cautious. It was in the darkness of night that he secretly met with Jesus:

Now there was a Pharisee named Nicodemus, a ruler of the Jews. He came to Jesus at night and said to him, "Rabbi, we know that you are a teacher who has come from God, for no one can do these signs that you are doing unless God is with him." Jesus answered and said to him, "Amen, amen, I say to you, no one can see the kingdom of God without being born from above." Nicodemus said to him, "How can a person once grown old be born again? Surely he cannot reenter his mother's womb and be born again, can he?" Jesus answered, "Amen, amen, I say to you, no one can enter the kingdom of God without being born of water and Spirit. What is born of flesh is flesh and what is born of spirit is spirit." JOHN 3:1–6

What did Nicodemus misunderstand in Jesus' answer to him?

Monologue

Nicodemus misunderstood the answer that Jesus gave. Jesus then explained more deeply what he meant. Jesus said:

"Amen, amen, I say to you, we speak of what we know and we testify to what we have seen, but you people do not accept our testimony. If I tell you about earthly things and you do not believe, how will you believe if I tell you about heavenly things? No one has gone up to heaven except the one who has come down from heaven, the Son of Man."   JOHN 3:11–13

Reflection

John then reflects on the meaning of the words of Jesus. He writes:

For God so loved the world that he gave his only Son, so that everyone who believes in him might not perish but might have eternal life. For God did not send his Son into the world to condemn the world, but that the world might be saved through him. Whoever believes in him will not be condemned, but whoever does not believe has already been condemned, because he has not believed in the name of the only Son of God. . . . But whoever lives the truth comes to the light, so that his works may be clearly seen as done in God.
                        JOHN 3:16–18, 21

In this Gospel story John the Evangelist uses the images of darkness and light. Nicodemus came in darkness (without faith), seeking to know Jesus better. The question is: Did he leave in the light (believing in Jesus)?

With a partner role-play Jesus' monologue. In your own words retell the message that Jesus gave to Nicodemus.

Understanding the Word of God

Darkness and Light

Whenever people encounter Jesus, their life changes in some way. At the burial of Jesus, John describes Nicodemus as "the one who had first come to him at night" (John 19:39). Why would Nicodemus be identified in this way?

Nicodemus journeyed from the dark into the light—out of secrecy into the open, from doubt to the truth, from unbelief to belief. Nicodemus's initial encounter with Jesus had a radical effect on him. It truly changed his life.

Explain how the images of darkness and light help us understand the Gospel account of the conversation between Jesus and Nicodemus.

Promise of Eternal Life

Jesus talked to Nicodemus about the new life one receives through water and the Holy Spirit. When we are reborn of the Holy Spirit, we have new life because of our faith in Christ. We receive the promise of **eternal life** with God. This is the very reason God sent his Son into the world. John writes:

> For God so loved the world that he gave his only Son, so that everyone who believes in him might not perish but might have eternal life.   JOHN 3:16

Christians have come to understand this rebirth through water and the Holy Spirit as Baptism. Through faith in Jesus and Baptism we are reborn as adopted sons and daughters of God. We journey out of the kingdom of darkness into God's marvelous light. We receive the promise that one day we will meet Christ and all the saints in the light of the heavenly kingdom.

FAITH CONNECTION

Using either a sequence of colors or words, describe a situation in which you have moved from darkness to light, or from doubt to truth.

OUR CHURCH
MAKES A DIFFERENCE

The Re-membering Church Ministry

Nicodemus came to Jesus in the darkness of night. Some Catholics find themselves in the "darkness." For one reason or another they have become inactive members of the Church. The Church reaches out to Catholics who are not actively taking part in the life of the Church and invites them into conversation. This ministry is sometimes called the re-membering ministry. Often these conversations take place during Lent.

People participating in the re-membering ministry of the Catholic Church often become spiritual companions. Spiritual companions walk together on their faith journey for a brief or extended period of time. Spiritual companions lead each other to new beginnings, to

a renewal of their lives in Christ. They help each other listen to the whisper of the Holy Spirit guiding their lives. Together they come to a renewed understanding of the Church. Spiritual companions help each other discover ways to live as faithful children of the Father.

The re-membering ministry of the Church is an example of one way people enter into conversation with Jesus. Whether they come in the darkness of the night or in the brightness of the noonday sun, they come seeking to discover the spiritual meaning of their lives. They seek to join once again in living their lives in Christ as faithful members of the Church.

When do you talk with others about Jesus? Explain why you find this easy or difficult to do.

WHAT DIFFERENCE
Does Faith Make in My Life?

Darkness into Light

Nicodemus visited Jesus at night. Secretly, he wanted to know who this Jesus was. So he took a risk, reached out in darkness, received the light of faith in Jesus, and became his follower. The Holy Spirit calls us out of the darkness of fear and invites us to take the risk to follow Jesus.

Fear can darken your life. It can paralyze you and it can hold you back. Fear can keep you from taking the risk to live as a true follower of Jesus Christ and become all he wants you to be.

On the other hand, fear is nothing to be afraid of. It can even be your friend. Fear can be good. It can be healthy and real. Fear can alert you to upcoming danger and make you aware of certain risks so you can make safe choices.

Fear is not good if it takes away your freedom to choose. Let's take a look at four basic human fears. You need to be aware of these fears and work at making them your friend and using them to achieve what is good. Otherwise, they can hold you back from living healthy relationships and being a courageous Christian. These fears are:

- fear of rejection
- fear of failure
- fear of pain
- fear of loss

Read the fears listed below. Identify each description of fear as either fear of rejection, fear of pain, fear of failure, or fear of loss. Check the ones that would keep you from making free choices or from taking the risks that are sometimes necessary to be a true disciple of Jesus.

❏ Afraid to be nice to someone new or to those not in your group.
_____

❏ Afraid to have a medical test if you think something is wrong.
_____

❏ Afraid to love someone deeply.
_____

❏ Afraid to say no to drugs.
_____

❏ Afraid to try out for a team.
_____

❏ Afraid to do the right thing if your friends choose to do something wrong.
_____

❏ Afraid of letting someone get to know the real you.
_____

❏ Afraid to tell your friends you are not going to the concert because you have to study.
_____

❏ Afraid to end an unhealthy relationship.
_____

❏ Afraid to talk about your relationship with God.
_____

Faith·
Decision

- Give an example of a fear that can have a positive effect on your life because it encourages you or challenges you to make good decisions.

- Give an example of how that same fear could keep you from taking the risk you need to take to make a good choice in your life.

This week I will look at a fear that is holding me back from living as a disciple of Jesus Christ. I will work on overcoming that fear by

_____
_____
_____
_____
_____

PRAY and REVIEW

"My Friends, Do Not Be Afraid"

Fear is a gift! It can encourage and strengthen us to seek to know Jesus better and live as his disciples.

All: **In the name of the Father, and of the Son, and of the Holy Spirit. Amen.**

Leader: Lord Jesus, we gather today to grow in hope and confidence by remembering your love for us.

All: **Amen.**

Reader 1: *Proclaim Luke 12:4–7.*

All: *Reflect silently on the reading. All come forward and place in a basket a folded paper on which they have written a fear or worry.*

Leader: Let us pray for the gifts of the Holy Spirit.

Reader 2: For the gifts of wisdom and understanding,

All: **Lord, hear our prayer.**

Reader 3: For the gifts of right judgment and courage,

All: **Lord, hear our prayer.**

Reader 4: For the gifts of knowledge and reverence,

All: **Lord, hear our prayer.**

Reader 5: For the gift of wonder and awe in your presence,

All: **Lord, hear our prayer.**

Leader: Father, send the Holy Spirit to strengthen us to live as faithful disciples of your Son.

All: **Amen.**

FAITH VOCABULARY

Use each of these faith words correctly in a sentence:

1. Sanhedrin
2. Pharisee
3. Torah
4. eternal life

MAIN IDEAS

Choose either (a) or (b) from each set of items. Write a brief paragraph to answer each of your choices.

1. (a) Describe what the Gospel tells us about Nicodemus.

   (b) Explain what Jesus told Nicodemus about being born from above.

2. (a) Discuss how the images of light and darkness help us understand the meaning of the Nicodemus story.

   (b) Compare the Nicodemus story with Baptism.

CRITICAL THINKING

Using what you have learned in this chapter, reflect on and explain this Scripture verse:

For God so loved the world that he gave his only Son, so that everyone who believes in him might not perish but might have eternal life.

JOHN 3:16

FAMILY DISCUSSION

What can we do as a family to celebrate our new life in Christ more courageously?

For more ideas on ways your family can live your faith, visit the "Faith First for Families" page at **www.FaithFirst.com**. Check out the "Make a Difference" activity.

Baptism and Confirmation

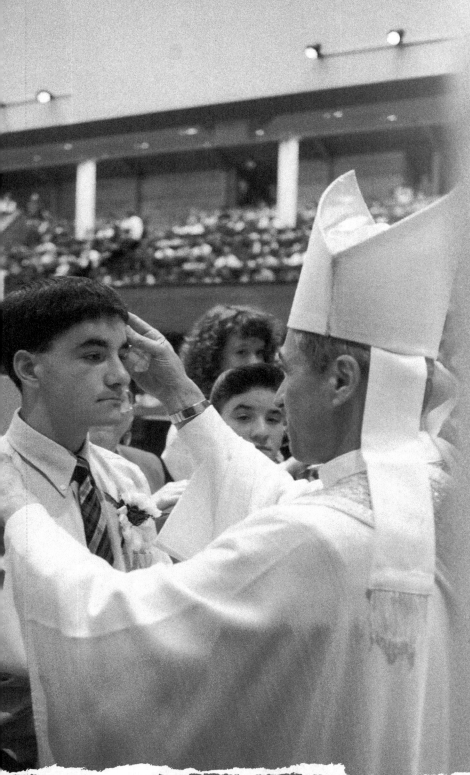

FAITH FOCUS

How do the Sacraments of Baptism and Confirmation change our lives?

FAITH VOCABULARY

Sacraments of Christian Initiation

Baptism

Confirmation

Into what groups have you been initiated? What were the ceremonies like?

The word *initiation* comes from the Latin word meaning "beginning." Sometimes we talk about being initiated into a group. We begin to be members of a group. In our Catholic faith, initiation has a very special meaning. It refers to the time when we begin new life in Jesus and his Body, the Church. The Sacraments of Christian Initiation make this new beginning possible.

What are the Sacraments of Christian Initiation?

Anointing with chrism, Rite of Confirmation

To each individual the manifestation of the Spirit is given for some benefit.
1 CORINTHIANS 12:7

Christian Initiation

Christian initiation is our entrance into the Church. Through the three **Sacraments of Christian Initiation** of Baptism, Confirmation, and Eucharist, we are joined to Christ and made sharers in his life. Because we are joined to Christ, we belong to his Body, the Church (see 1 Corinthians 12:27, Colossians 1:18).

Baptism is the beginning of our new life in Christ. Confirmation is its strengthening. Eucharist nourishes us with Christ's Body and Blood for our transformation in Christ. In this chapter we will study the first two of the three Sacraments of Christian Initiation, Baptism and Confirmation. The three Sacraments of Christian Initiation in some ways contain these three ideas.

An Initiation Is a New Beginning

Baptism, Confirmation, and Eucharist lay the foundation for the Christian life and mark a new beginning. They join us to Christ. By making us members of his Body, they also join us to the Church.

Baptism is the chief sacrament of forgiveness. This sacrament marks a new beginning by canceling, or wiping out, all sin in our lives, whether original sin or personal sins (see Acts of the Apostles 2:38).

Baptism at the Easter Vigil

Sponsors of the newly baptized holding candles lighted from Easter candle

Celebration of Baptism

You are very familiar with the celebration of Baptism. The essential parts of the celebration of this first sacrament include immersing a person three times into water (or pouring water three times over a person's head), while saying the words given to us by Christ:

(Name), I baptize you
in the name of the Father,
and of the Son,
and of the Holy Spirit.

RITE OF BAPTISM

Once a person is baptized he or she cannot receive Baptism again. This is because Baptism seals us with a spiritual character that marks us as forever belonging to Christ. It is a spiritual character that is indelible, that is, it cannot be removed or erased even by sin and is a permanent part of who we are. We belong to Christ forever.

Initiation Is a New Birth

Baptism is our birth into new life in Christ (see 1 Peter 1:23). In Baptism we receive the gift of the Holy Spirit, who enables us to believe in Christ and live the Gospel. Through the Holy Spirit, we become adopted sons and daughters of God the Father in the Son, Jesus. In other words, through Baptism we become adopted children of the Father, members of Christ's Body, and temples of the Holy Spirit (see 1 Corinthians 3:16, 6:19; 2 Corinthians 5:17; Ephesians 4:25).

The Door to the Other Sacraments

Baptism is the door or path to the other sacraments. We can only share in the other sacraments when we have been reborn of "water and the Holy Spirit." Only when we are joined to Jesus Christ in this basic way through Baptism can we meet him and be changed by him in the other sacraments.

FAITH CONNECTION

With a partner role-play a conversation with a friend who is being initiated into the Catholic Church. Share the responsibilities of being a Catholic. Write your ideas in this space.

_____

_____

_____

_____

Baptism Q and A

Baptism often generates questions from Catholics and non-Catholics alike. Here are some of the most frequently asked questions about Baptism and answers to them.

Question. Why are we baptized as infants in the Catholic Church? Why not wait until we can decide for ourselves?

Answer. From the earliest days of the Church's history, children have been baptized. Sharing in the life of Christ is such a remarkable and freely given gift of God that the Church wishes to share it with everyone.

Question. If Baptism is necessary for salvation, what happens to children who are not baptized?

Answer. The Church entrusts unbaptized children who die to God's mercy. Jesus' tenderness toward children allows us to trust that there is a way of salvation for God's unbaptized children.

Question. Are there unbaptized adults who are saved?

Answer. God has bound salvation to the Sacrament of Baptism, but he himself is not bound by his sacrament. The Church has always believed that those who die for their faith prior to being baptized are "baptized" by their death for and with Christ. Those preparing for Baptism who die before being baptized are assured of salvation by virtue of their desire to be baptized. Finally, all who are ignorant of Christ's Gospel and his Church and yet who seek God sincerely and strive to fulfill his will can be saved even if they have not been baptized.

Baptism of infant

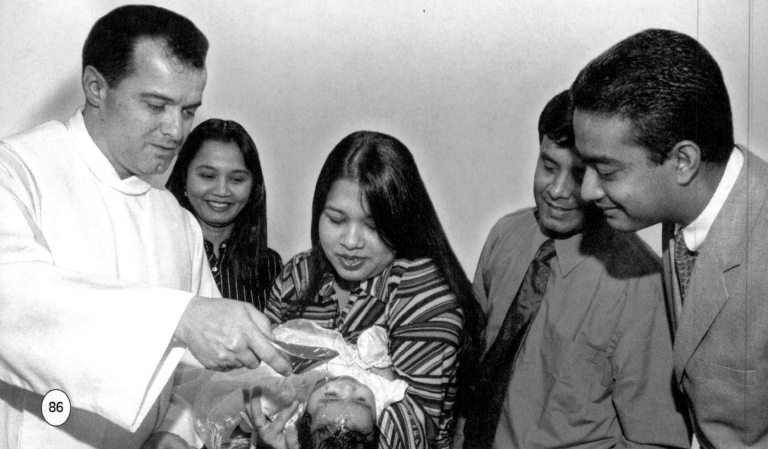

Question. Who can perform the sacrament of Baptism? Or, who is the minister of Baptism?

Answer. The ordinary minister of Baptism is a bishop, priest, or deacon. In cases of necessity, any person may baptize as long as that person performs the rite correctly and with proper intention to baptize someone into the Christian faith.

Question. Does the Catholic Church recognize Christians baptized in other Christian communities as truly baptized?

Answer. Yes, when those Christian communities follow the requirements for a proper celebration of Baptism. Baptism constitutes the foundation of the unity and communion among all Christians. We are all joined to Christ, the Head of the Church, the new People of God, through Baptism.

Question. Is the sacrament of Baptism ever celebrated together with other sacraments?

Answer. Yes. The Church celebrates the Rite of Christian Initiation with children of catechetical age (around age seven), older children, teens, and adults. This rite includes many steps and stages in the initiation process. These steps and stages culminate in the celebration of Baptism, Confirmation, and Eucharist at the Easter Vigil.

Why is it important to be baptized? What further questions do you have about the sacrament of Baptism?

Did you Know...

One part of the rite of Baptism is the clothing with the white garment. This is an outward sign of the new life in Christ received in Baptism. The white baptismal gown is sometimes the gown that has been worn by several generations of family members at their Baptisms. At Baptism you also receive a candle, which has been lighted from the Easter candle. This is a sign that through Baptism a person is enlightened by Christ. The baptized are to walk always as followers of Christ, the Light of the world, and keep the flame of faith alive in their hearts.

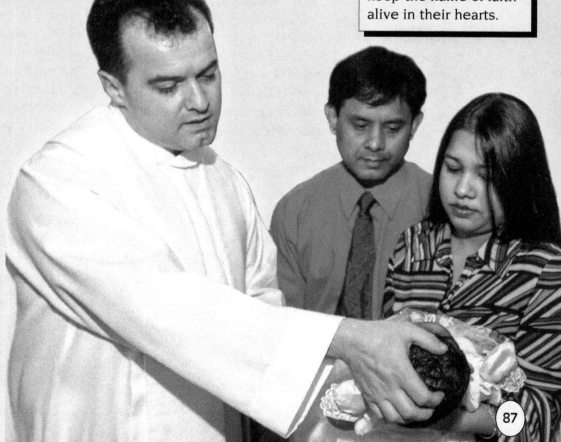

Anointing with chrism after Baptism

87

In Eastern rite Catholic Churches, the sacrament of Confirmation is administered to infants immediately after Baptism. The newly baptized and confirmed infant also receives Eucharist at this time. This tradition emphasizes the unity of the three Sacraments of Christian Initiation. In the Church in the West some people are confirmed as children or teens, still others as adults. At whatever age a baptized person receives Confirmation, the sacrament is always a gift from God. The grace of Confirmation does not depend on age.

Glass vessel containing chrism

Confirmation

Confirmation seals the sacramental graces of Baptism. It is the sacrament that celebrates the special gift of the Holy Spirit.

The Rite of Confirmation

The ordinary minister for Confirmation is a bishop. In some circumstances the local ordinary, or bishop of a diocese, delegates a priest to confer this sacrament. Whether Confirmation is administered by a bishop or by a priest, the essential rite of Confirmation includes laying the minister's hand on the head of the candidate for Confirmation and anointing the candidate's forehead with sacred chrism, saying, "Be sealed with the Gift of the Holy Spirit."

Candidates

All candidates for Confirmation who have attained the age of reason must profess their faith, be in a state of grace, and have the intention of receiving the sacrament. They must be prepared to assume the role of Christ's disciples and to give witness to their faith in Christ.

Effects of Confirmation

The effects, or sacramental graces, of the Church's celebration of Confirmation in the life of a baptized person are:

- Confirmation deepens our rebirth as adopted children of God the Father.
- Confirmation unites us more closely to the Lord Jesus.
- Confirmation increases the gifts of the Holy Spirit within us.
- Confirmation strengthens the bond of unity we experience with the Church.
- Confirmation strengthens us to spread and defend the faith by word and deed.

The special outpouring of the Holy Spirit that Confirmation represents brings the graces of Baptism to a new depth and fullness in the life of the believer. This is why the sacramental formula speaks of being *sealed* with "the Gift of the Holy Spirit." Without Confirmation, a person is not fully initiated into the Church. Like Baptism, Confirmation imprints an indelible spiritual mark, or character, on the soul, making it a once-in-a-lifetime experience.

FAITH CONNECTION

Look up and read one of these Scripture passages. Summarize what the Scripture you read teaches about living as a witness for Christ.

Matthew 16:24–27 • Mark 4:1–9 • Luke 4:16–22

_____

_____

_____

_____

OUR CHURCH
MAKES A DIFFERENCE

National Catholic Youth Conference

The People of God support one another in living their new life in Christ in many ways. Catholic teens in the United States of America support one another by coming together every year for the National Catholic Youth Conference.

The National Catholic Youth Conference (NCYC) is an extended weekend with speakers, musicians, and thousands of enthusiastic young people. Held in cities across the United States, the NCYC strives to emphasize these values: the dignity of each person, the gifts of young people, the call to justice and discipleship, and the wisdom of shared leadership.

All of this happens so that the Church can help young people rediscover that God is really and truly present in the world today and that he wants a relationship with them. Participation in a National Catholic Youth Conference widens the view of the Church for young people. They do this in many fun and dynamic ways.

Gathering together away from home can give us a fresh perspective on our faith. It can enliven our spirit and help us experience the laughter, joy, and prayer that our God wants us to experience in our daily lives.

How does gathering with others help us grow in faith?

89

WHAT DIFFERENCE
Does Faith Make in My Life?

Hospitality

At Baptism we are all welcomed into the family of God, the Church. In our own parish communities we welcome those who come to worship each week. How can we practice hospitality with others and be welcoming to people every day, not just on Sundays and holidays?

Hospitality, or the welcoming of people, is an attitude. It is a way of being that makes the people you greet feel comfortable and at home, and that they belong. Of course, sorry to say, in our society today we must always practice caution when we are dealing with total strangers. Let us talk specifically about the people we know at school, in our homes, in our neighborhoods, and in our parish communities.

Are You a Cordial, Welcoming Person?

Hospitality is a key characteristic of God's people. Ask yourself the following questions to determine just how hospitable and welcoming a person you are.

❖ When you pass someone in the hall from another grade, do you smile, say hello, or just ignore them?

❖ When someone new tries to sit with you at lunch, does he or she feel a warm reception or a cold shoulder?

❖ How do you treat the others outside your circle of friends? How inclusive or exclusive of people are you?

While you are not expected to be best friends with every single person in your school, you are expected to be a friendly, cordial, caring, inclusive person as Jesus was. Since God is present in everyone, when you welcome others, you welcome God. Here is a list of actions that you can do to grow as a welcoming person—a person of hospitality:

- ❖ Respect others.
- ❖ Accept others for who they are.
- ❖ Be courteous and considerate.
- ❖ Be generous, not possessive of your friends or your time.
- ❖ Be inclusive and invite someone new to join your circle of friends.
- ❖ Build up your self-esteem, but don't put others down or be jealous or push others away.

Faith Decision

- Imagine you are at a meeting of the student council. Brainstorm ideas for designing a program that welcomes new students. Identify key ideas that will make your program successful.

- This week I will reach out to a new student or a student I do not know very well. I will

_____

_____

_____

_____

_____.

PRAY and REVIEW

Professing Our Faith

Leader:

At Baptism we profess the faith of the Church and promise to live that faith. Each Easter Sunday we renew the promises we made in Baptism to serve God faithfully in his holy Catholic Church. Let us profess that faith again today.

Do you believe in God, the Father almighty, creator of heaven and earth?

All: I do.

Leader:

Do you believe in Jesus Christ, his only Son, our Lord, who was born of the Virgin Mary, was crucified, died, and was buried, rose from the dead, and is now seated at the right hand of the Father?

All: I do.

Leader:

Do you believe in the Holy Spirit, the holy catholic Church, the communion of saints, the forgiveness of sins, the resurrection of the body, and the life everlasting?

All: I do.

BASED ON PROFESSION OF FAITH, RITE OF BAPTISM

Leader:

God, our loving Father, send the Holy Spirit to teach us how to live as faithful followers of your Son, Jesus Christ. We ask this in his name.

All: Amen.

FAITH VOCABULARY

Define each of these faith terms:

1. Sacraments of Christian Initiation
2. Baptism
3. Confirmation

MAIN IDEAS

Choose either (a) or (b) from each set of items. Write a brief paragraph to answer each of your choices.

1. (a) Describe Christian initiation as a new beginning and a new birth.

   (b) Describe the essentials of the rite of Baptism.

2. (a) Describe the essentials of the rite of Confirmation.

   (b) Compare Baptism and Confirmation.

CRITICAL THINKING

Using what you have learned in this chapter, reflect on and explain this statement:
Baptism is the door or path to the other sacraments.

FAMILY DISCUSSION

How do we as a family give witness to our faith in Christ?

For more ideas on ways your family can live your faith, visit the "Faith First for Families" page at **www.FaithFirst.com**. Also check out the Teen Center for additional activities.

Eucharist

FAITH FOCUS

Why do we call the Eucharist both a sacrament and a sacrifice?

FAITH VOCABULARY

Eucharist   memorial

sacrifice

How might you react if Jesus visited your hometown?

What would happen if Jesus were to make a personal appearance in your hometown? Naturally, the media would go into a frenzy. News organizations from all over the world would crowd into your hometown. The fact of the matter is that Jesus is always present in the world. It's just that sometimes we don't look for him in the right places.

In what ways is Jesus present in the world today?

"This cup is the new covenant in my blood, which will be shed for you."

LUKE 22:20

Eucharist: Sacrament and Sacrifice

The Presence of Jesus

Jesus told his disciples that when two or three gathered in his name, he was there with them. He assured them:

> "I say to you, if two of you agree on earth about anything for which they are to pray, it shall be granted to them by my heavenly Father. For where two or three are gathered together in my name, there am I in the midst of them." MATTHEW 18:19–20

Jesus is always present with the Church. He is present with us when we celebrate the sacraments. He is present in a unique way when the Church celebrates the **Eucharist.**

The Eucharist is the sacrament of the Body and Blood of Christ, who is uniquely and really present under the appearances of bread and wine. Through the words and actions of this sacrament the bread and wine become the Body and Blood of Christ. We are made sharers in the Paschal Mystery of Christ. This is why we say the Eucharist is sacrament, memorial, and sacrifice.

The Eucharist as Sacrament

Christ is truly human and truly divine. He knew and knows well the human need to come to know spiritual, or unseen, realities through visible and concrete signs. The Eucharist as sacrament does just that. The Eucharist is the sacrament in which we receive the Body and Blood of Christ.

The Eucharist as Memorial

The Church celebrates the Eucharist in response to Jesus' command, "[D]o this in memory of me" (Luke 22:19). The Eucharist is a **memorial** of Christ's Paschal Mystery. The Eucharist does more than just recall or remember Jesus and his work. It makes Jesus really, truly, and substantially *present* with us. It makes it possible for us to take part in and share in the saving work of his salvation, his Paschal Mystery. Another way of saying this is: It gives us grace.

The Church uses the Greek word for *memory* to capture this mystery of faith. The word is *anamnesis*. At Eucharist we are with Christ, who is alive! Time and space are transcended. The work of Christ is not simply a work of the past that we are imagining is happening in the present. We are really sharing in the Paschal Mystery here and now!

Describe the Eucharist as sacrament and memorial.

The Eucharist as Sacrifice

At the Last Supper Jesus instituted the Eucharist. Joining with his disciples, Jesus ate the Passover meal with them. At the meal he did what they had always done—he blessed God, took, broke, and shared bread with them. He next took and gave them a cup of wine to drink from. At the Last Supper Jesus gave those actions new meaning. He said:

> "This is my body, which will be given for you; do this in memory of me. . . . This cup is the new covenant in my blood, which will be shed for you." LUKE 22:19–20

Jesus was linking this Passover supper with his **sacrifice** on the cross. The altar is a symbol of the sacrifice of Christ. Each celebration of the Eucharist is not a "new" sacrifice. It is a moment when we enter into and share in the timeless offering of the one sacrifice of Jesus Christ. Joined to Christ, the faithful become a living offering to God.

On the cross Jesus offered himself to the Father once and for all time. The Eucharist is a sacrifice because it *re-presents*, or makes present again, the sacrifice of Jesus on the cross. The Eucharist is offered for the forgiveness of sins and as reparation for the sins of the living and the dead.

Although Jesus truly died on the cross and was buried, he was raised from the dead to a new and glorified life. He ascended to the Father where he lives in glory. He continues his saving work in and with his Body, the Church, which Saint Peter the Apostle describes as a priestly people (see 1 Peter 2:9).

Jesus' priestly work did not come to an end when he returned to his Father. Jesus, our eternal High Priest, continues to offer his sacrifice to the Father and to intercede for us, his people.

Last Supper, woodcarving

FAITH CONNECTION

At Mass we pray, "May this sacrifice of our reconciliation, we pray, O Lord, advance the peace and salvation of all the world" (Eucharistic Prayer III). Describe what sacrifices you and your friends can make to continue Jesus' work in the world.

_____

_____

_____

_____

The Celebration of the Eucharist

The Eucharist is "the source and summit of the Christian life" (*Constitution on the Church* 11). In the Eucharist is found that which is the heart of the Church, Christ himself. The eucharistic celebration always includes certain elements that constitute one single act of worship.

The Celebrant

Christ, the ageless and perpetual High Priest, offers the eucharistic sacrifice. It is the same Christ, really and truly present with us under the appearances of bread and wine, who is offering the sacrifice. He gives and is given. By virtue of their ordination, priests, such as your parish priests, act in the person of Christ when they celebrate the Eucharist. The sacrament of Holy Orders consecrates and sets them apart for this unique ministry.

Liturgy of the Word

Taken from "the writings of the prophets" (the Old Testament) and "the memoirs of the apostles" (the New Testament), the word of God is proclaimed during every celebration of the Eucharist. By means of these Scripture readings as well as the homily and the Prayer of the Faithful, we receive and respond to the word of God.

Liturgy of the Eucharist

The eucharistic presence of Christ is accomplished when the elements of wheat bread and grape wine, the signs of the sacrament, are consecrated by a validly ordained priest. This consecration takes place during the Eucharistic Prayer. The priest asks the Father to send the Holy Spirit so that our offerings may become the Body and Blood of Christ. He prays:

Make holy, therefore, these
  gifts we pray,
by sending down your Spirit
  upon them like the dewfall,
so that they may become for us
the Body and Blood of our
  Lord Jesus Christ.

FROM ROMAN MISSAL,
EUCHARISTIC PRAYER II

Acting through the power of the Holy Spirit and in the name and Person of Jesus, the priest continues. First taking the bread and then the wine, he says and does what Jesus did and said at the Last Supper.

Christ's Body and Blood, his soul and divinity, the whole Person of Christ becomes truly and substantially present under the physical appearances of bread and wine. Saint John Damascene (ca. 675–ca. 749) summarized this great mystery of our faith. He wrote:

> You ask how the bread becomes the Body of Christ, and the wine . . . the Blood of Christ. I shall tell you: the Holy Spirit comes upon them and accomplishes what surpasses every . . . thought.
>
> FROM ON THE TRUE FAITH

Communion

We participate in the Eucharist most fully when we receive Christ's Body and Blood in Holy Communion. The Church recommends that we receive Holy Communion whenever we take part in the Mass and are rightly disposed, that is, we are unaware of any serious sin in our lives. We are obliged to receive Holy Communion at least once a year. The Church also encourages us to receive Christ under the forms of bread and wine. However, if we receive under only one form, we still receive Christ whole and entire.

Describe the main elements of the celebration of the Eucharist.

The Graces of the Sacrament of the Eucharist

By partaking of the Eucharist, we take part in Christ's friendship with us in many ways.

One with Christ. In the Eucharist Christ comes to us. Joined to Christ in Baptism, we are strengthened in our union with Christ. The Eucharist nourishes the unity in the Body of Christ.

Spiritual food. The Eucharist is spiritual food. Sharing the Eucharist preserves, increases, and renews the Holy Spirit's life of grace within us. It nourishes our communion with God and with one another.

Strength. Communion with Christ strengthens our ability to love and be loved. By frequently and regularly receiving the Eucharist, we are less inclined to give in to temptation and sin. The closer we stay to Christ and abide in his friendship, the more difficult it is to destroy that relationship through mortal sin.

Forgiveness. Receiving Holy Communion cleanses us from all sin except mortal sin. If we are aware of having committed grave, or mortal, sin, we must return to God's love and friendship in the sacrament of Reconciliation before we approach the eucharistic table to receive Holy Communion.

Commitment to the poor. Shortly after calling his disciples friends, Jesus commanded them to "love one another" (John 15:17). If we receive the Bread of Life but ignore those who need bread to live, we dishonor Christ's friendship.

Everlasting friendship. The Eucharist is Christ's pledge of his friendship in this world and forever in the next. He promises that one day all those who are faithful sons and daughters of God will see him and share in his glory.

Faith helps us see that God's revelation in the Old Covenant and in the New Covenant is one plan. At the Last Supper Jesus transformed the Passover meal into a memorial of his death and Resurrection. It became the new Passover meal, the Eucharist. Through the transforming power of the Holy Spirit, the faithful become a living offering to the Father. Joined to Christ and in unity with the Holy Spirit, we bless and give thanks to God the Father for his loving plan of creation and salvation.

FAITH CONNECTION

Choose one of the graces of the Eucharist. Create an image depicting that grace.

OUR CHURCH
MAKES A DIFFERENCE

Bread for the World

In October 1972, a small group of Catholics and Protestants met to discuss and reflect on how persons of faith could have an impact on the problem of hunger in the world. They wanted to do more than hand out food at the local food pantry, host a meal for the hungry, or take up an extra collection to buy food for families in need during the holidays. They talked and prayed about how they could tackle the problem of world hunger at its roots.

Today Bread for the World's 54,000 members work to eliminate the causes of hunger and poverty. They use the power they have as citizens in a democracy. Some of their efforts include encouraging the president to fight hunger at home and abroad through budgetary planning. They urged Congress to support the Hunger Relief Act of 1999 and support a dollar-an-hour increase in the minimum wage. Bread for the World is also striving to improve nutrition programs such as the food stamp program and school lunch and breakfast programs.

Bread for the World also coordinates efforts to reduce hunger worldwide. Many of these efforts focus on countries that year after year face cyclical poverty due to the large debt that their governments have. Bread for the World has joined with Pope John Paul II and Anglican Archbishop Desmond Tutu to seek meaningful, comprehensive debt relief. This is an important solution to the battle against massive poverty and hunger in countries around the world.

The members of Bread for the World believe that they can make this world a better place. They are serious in their efforts to follow Jesus' command to reach out to the thirsty and hungry in his name.

What do you do to live the Eucharist as you are sent forth to do at the end of Mass?

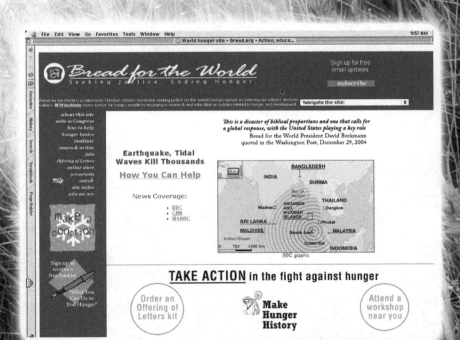

WHAT
DIFFERENCE
Does Faith Make in My Life?

Gratitude

Giving thanks to God is at the heart of the Eucharist. At the Eucharist we join with Christ in giving thanks and praise to God the Father. We give thanks and praise to the Father for all the blessings we have received and continue to receive through Christ his Son.

Giving thanks in words and actions puts the attitude of gratitude into action. Your attitude greatly influences the way you look at and respond to the world. It influences how you react emotionally to things. Your attitude even influences how your body responds physically. Your attitude affects your behavior and the choices you make.

The truth is, whether you are young or old, you need to be in touch with your attitude. You need to look at what is going on in your life, and at times make an attitude adjustment. By developing an attitude of gratitude you begin to recognize the many blessings and good things you have. You can avoid feeling sorry for yourself and being jealous or envious of others who seem to have more than you.

When you begin to see what you have and who you are, you express your gratitude to God for your life, your health, and your other gifts.

Some people, before they go to bed each night, write in their journal a list of things or events that happened that day for which they are grateful. Try it! You will come to appreciate and value that you are blessed. You will have a good night's sleep and wake up in the morning happier and ready to greet another new day—and share with everyone the good news of God's infinite generosity and kindness.

Faith Decision

- Discuss in a small group what this question means to you: When you see a glass 50 percent filled with water, do you see the glass half empty or half full?

- Complete an acrostic poem using the word *gratitude*. Share your acrostic with a partner.

G _____

R _____

A _____

T _____

I _____

T _____

U _____

D _____

E _____

This week I will choose to develop an attitude of gratitude by

_____

_____

_____.

PRAY and REVIEW

Celebrating Christ's Presence with Us

All:

**"(B)ehold, I am with you always,
until the end of the age."**

MATTHEW 28:20

Group 1:
Christ with me,
Christ before me,

Group 2:
Christ behind me,
Christ in me,

Group 1:
Christ beneath me,
Christ above me,

Group 2:
Christ on my right,
Christ on my left,

Group 1:
Christ in my breadth,
Christ in my length,
Christ in my height,
Christ in the mouth of everyone
who speaks to me,

Group 2:
Christ in the heart of everyone
who thinks of me,

Group 1:
Christ in every eye that
sees me,

Group 2:
Christ in every ear that
hears me.

All:

**"(B)ehold, I am with you always,
until the end of the age."**

MATTHEW 28:20

BASED ON PRAYER OF SAINT PATRICK

FAITH VOCABULARY

Define each of these faith terms:

1. Eucharist
2. memorial
3. sacrifice

MAIN IDEAS

Choose either (a) or (b) from each set of items. Write a brief paragraph to answer each of your choices.

1. (a) Explain what is meant by the real presence of Christ in the Eucharist.

   (b) Discuss the Eucharist as a sacrifice, a sacrament, or a memorial.

2. (a) Explain how the Eucharist strengthens our relationship with Jesus.

   (b) Explain how the Eucharist strengthens our relationship with all the faithful.

CRITICAL THINKING

Using what you have learned in this chapter, reflect on and explain this statement:
How holy this feast in which Christ is our food: his passion is recalled, grace fills our hearts, and we receive a pledge of the glory to come.

SAINT THOMAS AQUINAS

FAMILY DISCUSSION

How does sharing in the Eucharist strengthen the unity of our family?

For more ideas on ways your family can live your faith, visit the "Faith First for Families" page at **www.FaithFirst.com**. Also remember to read the next chapter of "Vista Falls Junior High" on the Teen Center.

Jesus Feeds Five Thousand

A Scripture Story

10

FAITH FOCUS

What is the meaning of the miracle of Jesus feeding five thousand people?

FAITH VOCABULARY

manna   Exodus
divine Providence

What other ways do you hear the word bread *used?*

The word *bread* is often used for things other than food. People sometimes say *bread* but mean *money*. In the Bible, bread is also used in many ways. Jesus called himself the Bread of Life.

What other Bible stories do you know that center around bread?

Miracle of the Five Thousand Feeding, stone containing mosaic of Chi-Rho (symbol for Jesus), fishes, loaves, and baskets containing fragments of bread, Dugit Beach, Sea of Galilee, near Tel Hadar, Israel

They all ate and were satisfied.
MARK 6:42

Bread in the Old Testament

The sacred writers of the Bible also gave the word *bread* a deeper meaning. Bread was often more than just a loaf of bread. They often broadened the meaning of the word *bread* to include food in general or eating. Other times, bread would have a more symbolic meaning. These are some of the symbolic meanings for the word *bread* found in the Old Testament.

- **Friendship.** Bread was often a sign of friendship. The Old Testament talks about eating and sharing bread with friends.

Abraham and the Three Angels, Eighteenth-century Greek icon

- **Hospitality.** Sharing bread is also a sign of showing people they are welcome in our homes. There are many stories in the Old Testament when bread is baked and served to strangers and other guests. For example: Sarah makes bread for the three strangers who visit Abraham (see Genesis 18:5–6). When Elijah visits the widow, she makes bread for him (see 1 Kings 17:7–16).

- **God's loving care.** The most well-known bread story in the Old Testament is God's feeding his people with **manna** in the desert. Manna was the breadlike food the Israelites ate during their **Exodus** journey through the desert (see Exodus 16:12–35).

In the hungriest moments of their journey when their survival seemed very doubtful, God was there—faithful to them. Their faith and trust in God got the Israelites through this crisis and every other crisis of their journey.

Describe the deeper meanings the sacred writers of the Old Testament gave to the word bread.

The Gathering of the Manna.
James J. Tissot (1836–1902), French painter.

Bread in the Gospel

The sacred writers of the New Testament knew and understood the long tradition of the use of bread as a symbol in the Old Testament. Building on these meanings, the Evangelists included bread and meal stories in their accounts of the Gospel. This helped their listeners and readers to understand the deeper meaning of what Jesus was teaching.

- **Friendship and hospitality.** In the Bible, sharing bread and a meal was often a sign of friendship and hospitality. Many of the great teachings of Jesus took place when he was at table with people. Jesus ate not only with his disciples and friends but also with Pharisees and others who strongly objected to his teachings. God invites all people to live in friendship with him.

- **God's care.** Jesus taught his disciples to pray:

  "Our Father in heaven, . . . Give us today our daily bread." MATTHEW 6:9, 11

This use of the symbol of bread reminded his disciples that God the Father cares for us. He is the source of all our blessings, spiritual and physical. We should place our trust in him (see Matthew 6:25–34).

- **Bread from heaven.** Jesus used the word *bread* to help his followers come to know who he was. After referring to the Exodus story of the Israelites eating manna in the desert, he said, "I am the bread of life" (John 6:35).

Christ in the House of Martha and Mary, pastel on paper. Rene-Marie Castaing (1896–1944), French artist.

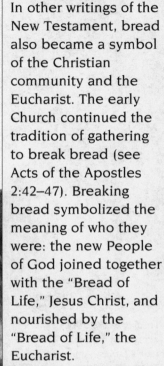

Did you Know...

In other writings of the New Testament, bread also became a symbol of the Christian community and the Eucharist. The early Church continued the tradition of gathering to break bread (see Acts of the Apostles 2:42–47). Breaking bread symbolized the meaning of who they were: the new People of God joined together with the "Bread of Life," Jesus Christ, and nourished by the "Bread of Life," the Eucharist.

FAITH CONNECTION

Some families place great value on family meals. What might their reasons be?

_____

_____

_____

Reading the Word of God

Feeding of the 5000, acrylic on canvas. Laura James, American contemporary artist.

The Multiplication of Loaves and Fishes. Michael Wolgemuth (1434–1519), German painter.

"Give Them Some Food"

One time Jesus had been teaching and curing people. Many were attracted to him because of what he was saying and doing. Others were not. Some came to believe in him. Others did not. A few became hostile to him.

Getting into a boat with his disciples, Jesus crossed the Sea of Tiberias, which is actually a very large lake and also called the Sea of Galilee. When they reached the other side, Jesus saw a large crowd that had walked around the lake to meet him. It could have been a very long walk. The Sea of Tiberias is thirteen miles long and eight miles wide at its widest point.

This is what Mark the Evangelist tells us happened when Jesus and his disciples saw the crowd.

When he disembarked and saw the vast crowd, his heart was moved with pity for them, for they were like sheep without a shepherd; and he began to teach them many things. By now it was already late and his disciples approached him and said, "This is a deserted place and it is already very late. Dismiss them so that they can go to the surrounding farms and villages and buy themselves something to eat." He said to them in reply, "Give them some food yourselves." But they said to him, "Are we to buy two hundred days' wages worth of food and give it to them to eat?" He asked them, "How many loaves do you have? Go and see." And when they had found out they said, "Five loaves and two fish." So he gave orders to have them sit down in groups on the green grass. The people took their places in rows by hundreds and by fifties. Then, taking the five loaves and the two fish and looking up to heaven, he said the blessing, broke the loaves, and gave them to [his] disciples to set before the people; he also divided the two fish among them all. They all ate and were satisfied. And they picked up twelve wicker baskets full of fragments and what was left of the fish. Those who ate [of the loaves] were five thousand men.

MARK 6:34–44

Jesus saw the crowd and had pity for the people. The trip that the people in the crowd made to follow him was not an easy trip. They were tired and hungry. Jesus fed them.

Imagine yourself as a member of the crowd in this story. Describe your understanding of the meaning of what just happened.

Miracle of the Loaves and Fishes. James J. Tissot (1836–1902), French painter.

God's Caring Presence Among Us

The Church continues to see in this Gospel story Jesus' revelation that God is always present with us, caring for us. The Church calls the loving, caring presence of God among us **divine Providence.**

Connection with the Church

The Gospel account of the multiplication of the loaves and fish also reflects the early Church's faith in the Eucharist. After all the people had eaten, the disciples picked up the fragments of bread and what remained of the fish. The word

fragments is found in early Christian writings to describe the pieces of broken bread at the Eucharist. This Gospel passage passes on to us the early Church's belief that Jesus is always present with us and nourishes us in the Eucharist. Jesus is the Bread of Life (see John 6:48).

Connection with Eternal Life

Christians have come to understand that this Gospel passage also points to the future life in God's kingdom. We see this more closely when we read Jesus' teaching in John 6:22–71. In this teaching, which is called "The Bread of Life Discourse," Jesus says:

> "I am the bread of life. Your ancestors ate the manna in the desert, but they died; this is the bread that comes down from heaven so that one may eat it and not die." JOHN 6:48–50

The Eucharist is our pledge of future glory. It reminds us of the joy we will share at the heavenly banquet at the end of time.

FAITH CONNECTION

Check which of these caring things you do. Then describe how you are a sign of God's caring presence among us when you do that work.

❑ *Help a classmate at school who is having difficulty with a subject.*

❑ *Join with other youth on a parish mission project.*

❑ _____

(your own example)

OUR CHURCH
MAKES A DIFFERENCE

The H.U.G.S. Truck

The H.U.G.S. (Hearts United Giving & Sharing) Truck ministry of Saint Mark the Evangelist Catholic Community is a clear sign of God's loving, caring presence among us. It is a very practical demonstration of how one parish shows its solidarity with the Church's poor—month after month, year after year.

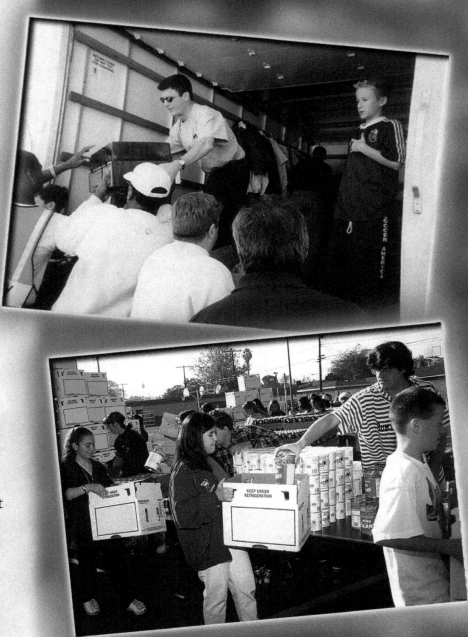

Each month the people of Saint Mark's parish collect canned food, used clothing, used furniture, and other everyday items like soap, shampoo, and school supplies. The collection takes place after each Mass on an assigned Sunday. The goods that are collected are loaded onto a truck and immediately transported to a parish that the people of Saint Mark's have committed to help on a regular basis.

Saint Mark's H.U.G.S. Truck ministry represents a massive effort to help others. It is important to point out that this generous spirit consists of material realities as well as spiritual realities. The spiritual dimension of this ministry consists of reflecting on how to use one's time and talents to best live the Gospel and serve the kingdom of God.

What are some other examples of parish ministry to the needy? How can you become involved in helping other people?

WHAT DIFFERENCE
Does Faith Make in My Life?

Sharing Our Blessings

Jesus taught that all his disciples are to share their blessings with others. Whether we are wealthy or poor, Jesus asks us to share our resources, especially with those in need. The truth is, whether you have a lot of material things or hardly any at all, you do have certain gifts and talents that you are asked to share with those in need.

If we all share whatever resources we have, we all win. As followers of Jesus we help others come to know God's great love and care for them, and we will come to know more deeply God's love and goodness in our own lives.

Share Who You Are

Here are examples of some gifts and talents you may have that you can generously share with others.

I can share my gifts of:

 generosity

I can do someone a favor, or do a kind deed.

 intelligence

I can tutor someone who needs help in a certain subject.

 time

I can talk to, listen to, or help someone who needs a friend.

Name and explain other gifts you can share.

I can share my talents of:

 singing or dancing

I can entertain someone, or cheer them up.

 playing sports

I can help coach younger children.

 cooking

I can help my family by preparing a special meal or a dessert.

Name and explain other talents you can share.

_____

_____

_____

_____

Faith·
Decision

- In a small group identify ways that people who live in poverty can be generous sharers of their gifts and talents.

- Discuss what it means to say that it is better to give than to receive.

This week I can be a generous giver and sharer of my gifts and talents by

_____

_____

_____

_____

_____

PRAY and REVIEW

A Prayer for God's People

Leader: Praying for others is one way we show our caring love for them. Let us pray for people in need so that they may come to know and trust in God's caring presence among them.

Lord God, Father of all, look lovingly on your people.

Reader: Bless your Church with the spirit of generosity and mercy so she may serve all those in need,

All: **Lord, hear us.**

Reader: Bless our nation with the spirit of compassion and kindness to reach out and share her blessings with the poorest among us,

All: **Lord, hear us.**

Reader: Bless people who are suffering spiritually and physically with the strength of your healing love,

All: **Lord, hear us.**

Reader: Bless people who are hungry and are in need of shelter with the gift of people who share their blessings with them,

All: **We pray you, hear us.**

Reader: Bless *(all privately add their personal petitions),*

All: **Lord, hear us.**

Leader: God our Father,
in Jesus Christ, your Son,
your caring love for us was
    most fully revealed.
May we always trust in
    that love.

All: **Amen.**

FAITH VOCABULARY

Use each of the faith terms *manna*, *Exodus*, and *divine Providence* correctly in a sentence.

MAIN IDEAS

Choose either (a) or (b) from each set of items. Write a brief paragraph to answer each of your choices.

1. (a) Describe some of the meanings for the word *bread* that are found in the Old Testament.

   (b) Describe some of the meanings for the word *bread* that are found in the Gospels.

2. (a) Explain how the Gospel account of Jesus feeding the crowd with the bread and fish helped the early Church understand the Eucharist.

   (b) Connect the Gospel account of Jesus feeding the crowd with the gift of eternal life.

CRITICAL THINKING

Using what you have learned in this chapter, reflect on and explain this statement:
    We should share, not only out of our abundance, but out of who we are.

FAMILY DISCUSSION

What family blessings will our family share with people in need in the community we live in?

For more ideas on ways your family can live your faith, visit the "Faith First for Families" page at **www.FaithFirst.com**. Also click on the Teen Center and read about the saint of the week.

Anointing of the Sick and Penance and Reconciliation

11

FAITH FOCUS

How is the Church a sign and instrument of Christ's healing in the world?

FAITH VOCABULARY

Sacraments of Healing

concupiscence

Penance and Reconciliation

Anointing of the Sick

conversion

seal of confession

In your opinion, what are the greatest examples of suffering in the world?

Television news shows are constantly filled with stories of suffering. God knows the suffering that is going on in our world. Jesus himself personally suffered. He also reached out to people who were suffering and touched their lives with God's healing touch.

How does the Church respond to the many forms of suffering in the world?

Jesus stretched out his hand, touched him, and said, ". . . Be made clean."

LUKE 5:13

God's Healing Love

The Sacraments of Healing

Suffering, whether it is physical, emotional, or spiritual, can bring us to our knees. It can make us vulnerable and powerless. It is often during such times that we find ourselves turning to God and placing our hope and trust in him.

The Catholic Church continues Jesus' ministry of reaching out to people who suffer through the **Sacraments of Healing**—Anointing of the Sick and Penance and Reconciliation. The Church is a sign and instrument of Jesus' healing. Through the power of the Holy Spirit the Church will continue that work until the end of time when Christ will return in glory.

Anointing of the Sick

Jesus' compassion and ministry with the sick and dying (see Matthew 9:35) are made present in the Church through the sacrament of **Anointing of the Sick** (see James 5:13–14). This sacrament confers the grace of strengthening our faith and trust in God. We receive the grace to face our sickness, weakness, or dying with courage and hope.

Celebrating the Sacrament

The Church celebrates Anointing of the Sick with the faithful of all ages—young people, adults, and the elderly—who are seriously ill or weak. Only bishops and priests can administer the sacrament of Anointing of the Sick.

The ritual for celebrating this sacrament is simple. Its principal elements are:
- the invocation of the Holy Spirit effected by the priest's silent laying on of hands,
- the prayers of intercession, and
- the anointing on the forehead and hands of the sick person with the blessed oil of the sick.

Anointing of the Sick can be received each time a Christian falls seriously ill. It can also be celebrated more than once during the same illness if that illness worsens.

Explain the essentials of the rite of Anointing of the Sick.

Effects, or Graces, of the Sacraments

Anointing of the Sick, like each of the sacraments, confers special graces, or makes us sharers in its own way in the Paschal Mystery of Christ. Some of the graces of this sacrament are:

- God assures the grace of peace and courage to strengthen individuals to overcome any difficulties associated with serious illness and old age.
- This sacrament provides healing for the soul and sometimes healing for the body.
- This sacrament grants forgiveness of sins if the sick person is unable to receive forgiveness through the celebration of the sacrament of Reconciliation.

- This sacrament unites the sick person more closely to Christ's Passion. The person's suffering becomes a participation in Jesus' saving work.

- In cases when death is imminent, this sacrament prepares the person for the final journey into eternal life.

If you have ever been seriously ill, you may have realized more deeply the importance of your faith and your friendship with Jesus. Celebrating Anointing of the Sick strengthens that faith and helps us realize that God is present with us in our times of illness and weakness.

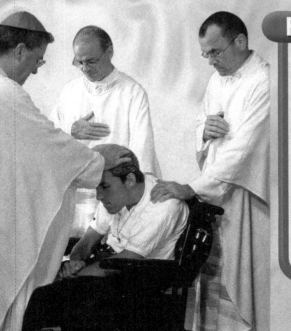

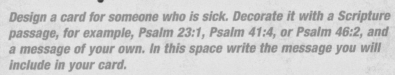

FAITH CONNECTION

Design a card for someone who is sick. Decorate it with a Scripture passage, for example, Psalm 23:1, Psalm 41:4, or Psalm 46:2, and a message of your own. In this space write the message you will include in your card.

_____

_____

_____

_____

Conversion

There is another kind of healing that all of us need because of our fallen nature. Everyone suffers from the effects of original sin. Something within us seems to call us away from trusting in God's love. Something tries to turn our heart away from that love. This is called **concupiscence.** Concupiscence is the inclination to sin that is a result of original sin.

When we give in to this inclination to sin, the Holy Spirit calls us back to friendship with God and his people, the Church. We call this movement of turning our heart back to God's love **conversion.**

The Sacrament of Penance and Reconciliation

Jesus gave his Church the authority to forgive sins (see John 20:21–23; Matthew 16:19). When we sin after we have been baptized, we have the opportunity to have our broken friendship with God and the Church healed through celebrating the sacrament of **Penance and Reconciliation.**

Reconciliation is the sacrament through which we receive forgiveness of sins we have committed after Baptism by the sincere confessing of our sins to a priest to whom the power to forgive sins has been given by the authority of Jesus and of the Church.

There are four essential elements to the proper celebration of the sacrament of Penance and Reconciliation. They are:

Contrition

Contrition is true sorrow for sins arising from our faith in God and love for him. True sorrow includes the desire not to sin again. Sorrow arising from love for God is called perfect contrition. Sorrow arising from other motives, such as the trouble sin has caused or the fear of discovery or the fear of punishment, is called imperfect contrition.

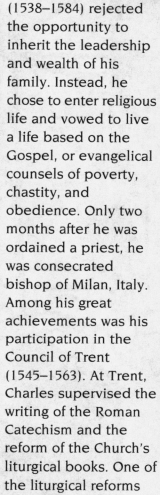

Confession

Confession is stating our sins to a bishop or priest who, by his ordination, has the power to forgive sins in the name of Jesus Christ. We must confess all mortal sins we have not yet confessed. Church law requires us to confess our mortal sins at least once a year. The confession of venial sins, while not necessary, is still highly recommended by the Church.

If you have any worries that the priest will tell others about your sins, put your fears to rest. Priests are under the **seal of confession.** This means that priests are bound to keep absolute secrecy regarding all sins confessed to them.

Satisfaction

Satisfaction means making up for our sins. We make satisfaction by accepting and performing the penance the priest assigns. We have an obligation and responsibility to make reparation for our sins, or repair the damage caused by them. Performing this penance helps repair the harm caused by sin. It also helps us develop habits to live as followers of Christ.

Absolution

Absolution is forgiving, or freeing, us from our sins. The words of absolution make it clear that the power to forgive sins is God's alone, celebrated in the Church's ministry of healing.

Describe the four elements necessary for the celebration of the sacrament of Reconciliation.

Effects, or Graces, of the Sacrament of Penance and Reconciliation

The sacrament of Penance and Reconciliation, like Anointing of the Sick and the other sacraments, has its own special effects, or graces. Some of the graces of this sacrament are:

- Reconciliation restores us to the relationship of love with God that we entered into at Baptism.

- This sacrament restores us and heals any wounds we inflicted on the Body of Christ.

- All sin has consequences. Mortal sin has deadly, or eternal, consequences. Celebrating Reconciliation remits, or takes away, eternal punishment that is the consequence of mortal sin.

- One of the consequences of sin is that it weakens our love for God. We must correct this consequence by being purified of sin and strengthened in our relationship with God either here on earth or after we die. Celebrating Penance and Reconciliation accomplishes this remission of temporal, or temporary, punishment either in part or entirely.

- Knowing and receiving God's forgiveness is a source of peace of mind.

- We receive the spiritual strength to live faithfully as children of God.

FAITH CONNECTION

Think about a moment of conversion in your life. Write and then pray a prayer of thanksgiving to God for helping you grow in your friendship with him.

_____

_____

_____

OUR CHURCH
MAKES A DIFFERENCE

Ministering with the Sick

At Mass we pray for those who are sick and dying. We pray for family members who are ill. We hear television reporters inviting people to pray during national tragedies. What difference does this all make? Well, apparently enough that the world is now paying attention to the healing power of prayer.

Ministers to the Sick

Many of the faithful—priests, deacons, religious brothers and sisters, and laypeople—live out their vocation by ministering with and praying for the sick. Some work full- or part-time at hospitals or long-term care homes with patients and pray with and for them. Others volunteer to visit with and pray for people who are sick at local hospitals, nursing homes, or other health-care facilities.

Prayer and Healing

Many of us have experienced healing in one way or another in our lives. We are forgiven by someone we have hurt. We forgive ourselves when we realize that we are human and make mistakes. We seek forgiveness from others and God, and promise to make better decisions in the future. We experience healing every day in some way— if we let ourselves. What is it about our belief that creates healing in others and ourselves?

Prayer and faith make a difference. The fact is that 43 percent of doctors regularly pray for their patients. We also know that, on average, people with a strong religious commitment have better overall health. They live longer too.

Who is in need of healing that you will pray for this week? Take a moment now and pray for that person or those people.

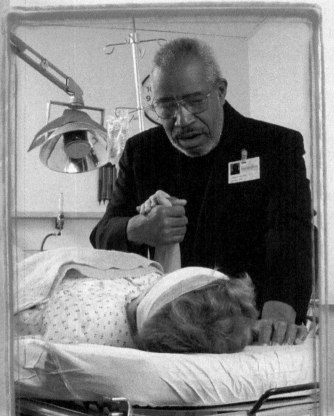

119

WHAT DIFFERENCE
Does Faith Make in My Life?

Forgiving and Healing

The sacraments of Reconciliation and Anointing of the Sick are part of the foundation for living a Christian life. Jesus practiced a lifetime of forgiveness. Through God's love we are called to forgiveness, conversion, and healing. God asks us to forgive one another as he forgives us.

Some people think forgiving is easy. They say things like "Forgive and forget" and "Time heals all wounds." Other people believe if we just ignore the hurt, it will go away.

Why is it so hard for us to really forgive and let go of hurt and pain?

When people hurt us, there is a part of us that wants to get even, to seek revenge and hurt back. Jesus knew that forgiveness is a very difficult human thing to do. Jesus also both showed us how to forgive by the way he forgave (see Luke 23:24) and commanded us to forgive (see Matthew 6:14–15 and 18:21–22).

Forgiveness Is Not

It is important to know what forgiveness is not. It is not necessarily about:

▲ saying it is okay that the other person hurt you.

▲ pretending it didn't hurt; saying it really didn't bother you when it did.

▲ forgetting about it.

▲ punishing the other person, or getting even.

▲ being a victim.

When you hold on to hurt or grudges, it is painful. It drains your energy, your happiness, your spontaneity, and your dreams.

Steps to Forgiveness and Healing

Jesus lived a lifetime of forgiveness. Here are some steps to help you live a life of forgiveness and healing:
▲ Pray and ask the Holy Spirit to open your mind and heart so that you can forgive.

- Name the hurt, or whatever the person did to you.
- Feel the feelings. Know that the feelings are normal. Do not avoid them.
- Talk to the person who hurt you. If that is not possible, talk to a trusted friend or parent. Sharing pain can help diminish it.
- Write a letter to the person and express exactly how you feel. (You will not mail this letter, and it may take a few letters until you feel better.) Then rip up the letter and throw it away. Writing can help you release some feelings.
- Let go when you can. This means make a choice, a real decision, to forgive. *Forgive* is a verb. It is an action word. It is something you do. Holding on to negative feelings continues to hurt you over and over again. Let go of these feelings.
- Move on. Forgiving is the best gift you can give yourself. It is what Jesus asks you to do, and it will lead to your own healing.

Faith· Decision

- In small groups brainstorm a list of words and phrases that express forgiveness and healing.

- Design a cover for a CD of songs of healing and forgiveness. Use the words and phrases you brainstormed to create titles for the songs on the CD.

This week I will choose to forgive by

_____

_____

_____

_____

_____ .

PRAY and REVIEW

The Jesus Prayer

Jesus taught that we do not need to use many words when we pray. God knows what is in our hearts and on our minds before we share our feelings and thoughts with him. The Jesus Prayer is a simple form of prayer based on the Gospel story of Jesus healing the man born blind that uses few words.

Leader:

Saint Paul encourages us to pray often. He wrote: "Pray without ceasing" (1 Thessalonians 5:17). Quietly pray the words "Jesus, have mercy on me" (Luke 18:38).

All:

(Close your eyes, take a deep breath, and say the name)

Jesus,

(Pause briefly, exhale, and say)

have mercy on me.

(Repeat the prayer slowly several times.)

FAITH VOCABULARY

Define each of these faith terms:

1. Sacraments of Healing
2. Anointing of the Sick
3. concupiscence
4. conversion
5. Penance and Reconciliation
6. seal of confession

MAIN IDEAS

Choose either (a) or (b) from each set of items. Write a brief paragraph to answer each of your choices.

1. (a) Describe the celebration of the sacrament of Anointing of the Sick.

   (b) Name the effects of celebrating Anointing of the Sick.

2. (a) Describe the celebration of the sacrament of Penance and Reconciliation.

   (b) Name the effects of celebrating Penance and Reconciliation.

CRITICAL THINKING

Using what you have learned in this chapter, reflect on and explain this statement: No one ever suffers alone.

FAMILY DISCUSSION

What things can we do as a family to heal the harm and hurts we may cause one another?

For more ideas on ways your family can live your faith, visit the "Faith First for Families" page at **www.FaithFirst.com**. Also check out the most recent games on the Teen Center.

Matrimony and Holy Orders

12

FAITH FOCUS

How do the sacraments of Matrimony and Holy Orders serve the Church, the new People of God?

FAITH VOCABULARY

Sacraments at the Service of Communion

Holy Orders

Matrimony

How do you see people serving one another?

Have you ever asked yourself, "What does God want from me?" Christians find the answers to that question in Christ. At the Last Supper, Jesus wrapped a towel around his waist and washed his disciples' feet. Making sure that no one missed the real meaning of what he was doing, Jesus said, "[A]s I have done for you, you should also do" (John 13:15).

How does the Church follow Jesus' example today?

"[A]s I have done for you, you should also do."
JOHN 13:15

Called to Serve the Church

Sacraments at the Service of Communion

Christians live our lives in Christ, serving others as Jesus did. The Holy Spirit invites some members of the Church to help and guide the Church in living a life of service in Christ in a unique way. They are consecrated, or set aside, for this holy work in the two **Sacraments at the Service of Communion—**Holy Orders and Matrimony.

Marriage

From the very beginning a man and a woman were created as partners to share their lives in faithful love (see Genesis 2:24). God himself has endowed marriage with a number of essential qualities that are at the foundation of marriage. Marriage is:

A covenant. Marriage is a relationship of love that a man and a woman freely and knowingly enter into with each other. Created in the image and likeness of God, married couples become living signs of the Covenant God entered into with humankind.

Permanent, or indissoluble. God's covenant with his people is permanent. It is unbreakable, or indissoluble, and permanent by its very nature.

Faithful and exclusive. The marriage covenant is lifelong and requires faithfulness and exclusivity on the part of married spouses. Polygamy and adultery are contrary to these two essential qualities of marriage. Polygamy is having more than one spouse at the same time. When a married man or woman has sexual relations or the desire for sexual relations with another partner, he or she commits adultery.

Openness to children. The willingness of a married couple to receive marriage's "supreme gift," a child, is at the heart of married love (see Genesis 1:28). Married couples are to responsibly plan the growth and development of their family life. Using means of birth control that are not natural is contrary to this essential quality of marriage, openness to children.

Why do we call marriage a covenant?

The Sacrament of Matrimony

The sacrament of **Matrimony** celebrates the marriage between a baptized man and a baptized woman. This sacrament sets apart and strengthens the married couple to live as a sign of the unity and love between Christ and his Church. They are called and receive the grace to be a mirror of God's love for us and of Christ's love for his Church. Matrimony gives the spouses the grace to love each other with the love with which Christ loves his Church.

The Marriage Promises

The essential element of this sacrament is the couple's exchange of marriage promises. The woman and man themselves are the ministers of this sacrament. The priest or deacon receives the consent of the couple on behalf of the whole Church and gives the married couple the Church's blessing. Since Matrimony consecrates the couple to openly and publicly serve the whole Church, this sacrament is appropriately celebrated at Mass in the presence of the worshiping assembly, which has gathered for the celebration.

Divorce and Remarriage

Divorce is the breaking up of a true marriage that has been freely and knowingly entered into.

Divorce is totally opposed to God's plan and the teaching of Jesus (see Matthew 19:6). The Church cannot change this teaching.

Catholics who divorce and remarry without an annulment from the Church are not separated from the Church. While such individuals cannot receive Holy Communion, they are still members of the Body of Christ, the Church, and are called to lead Christian lives and educate their children in the faith.

Christian married couples are living signs of the new and everlasting Covenant made in Christ with the human family. Through this new and everlasting Covenant all people share in the very life of the Holy Trinity.

Compare marriage and the sacrament of Matrimony.

Did you Know...

An annulment is a judgment by the Church that the marriage entered into by a couple was never a sacramental marriage. This means that one of the essential qualities of marriage was never part of the covenant the couple promised to live.

FAITH CONNECTION

List examples of contemporary images of marriage promoted by the media. Mark a ✔ if an image reflects the Church's teaching, or mark an ✗ if an image is contrary to the Church's teaching. Share the reasons for your choices.

☐ _____   ☐ _____

☐ _____   ☐ _____

☐ _____   ☐ _____

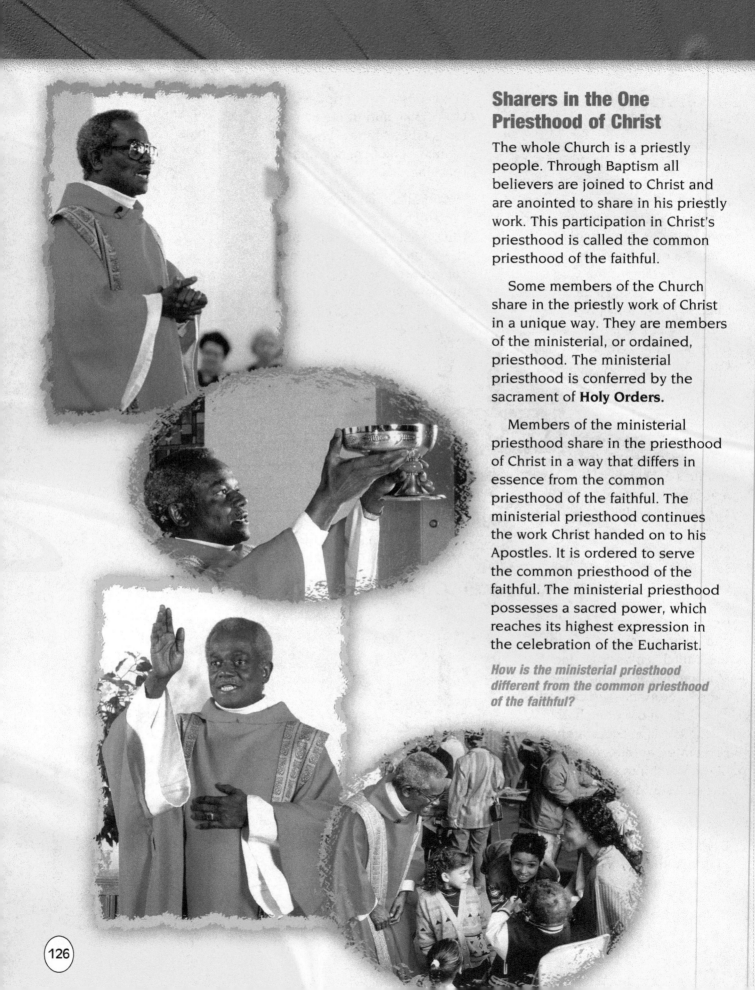

Sharers in the One Priesthood of Christ

The whole Church is a priestly people. Through Baptism all believers are joined to Christ and are anointed to share in his priestly work. This participation in Christ's priesthood is called the common priesthood of the faithful.

Some members of the Church share in the priestly work of Christ in a unique way. They are members of the ministerial, or ordained, priesthood. The ministerial priesthood is conferred by the sacrament of **Holy Orders.**

Members of the ministerial priesthood share in the priesthood of Christ in a way that differs in essence from the common priesthood of the faithful. The ministerial priesthood continues the work Christ handed on to his Apostles. It is ordered to serve the common priesthood of the faithful. The ministerial priesthood possesses a sacred power, which reaches its highest expression in the celebration of the Eucharist.

How is the ministerial priesthood different from the common priesthood of the faithful?

The Sacrament of Holy Orders

In the sacrament of Holy Orders a baptized man becomes a member of the order of bishops, priests, or deacons. The ministries imparted by Holy Orders are indispensable for the essential makeup of the Church. Without bishops, priests, and deacons, we really cannot speak of the Church.

Rite of Ordination

Only Church authority has the right and responsibility to call baptized men to receive the sacrament of Holy Orders. Ultimately, however, it is Christ who bestows the sacrament. He does so through his bishops, who are the successors to the Apostles and receive the fullness of the sacrament of Holy Orders.

The sacrament of Holy Orders is conferred in all three degrees by a bishop. This is done by the laying on of hands on the man being ordained, followed by a solemn prayer of consecration asking God to grant the ordinand, or man being ordained, the graces of the Holy Spirit required for his ministry. In part the bishop at the ordination of a priest prays:

> **Almighty Father,**
> **grant to these servants of yours**
> **the dignity of the priesthood.**
> **Renew within them the Spirit**
> **of holiness.**

> **As co-workers with**
> **the order of**
> **bishops**
> **may they be faithful**
> **to the ministry**
> **that they receive**
> **from you,**
> **Lord God,**
> **and be to others a**
> **model of right**
> **conduct.**
>
> **May they be faithful**
> **in working with the**
> **order of bishops,**
> **so that the words**
> **of the Gospel may**
> **reach the ends**
> **of the earth,**
> **and the family**
> **of nations,**
> **made one in Christ,**
> **may become God's**
> **one, holy people.**
> **FROM PRAYER OF**
> **CONSECRATION**

Like those who receive Baptism and Confirmation, the ordinand is imprinted with an indelible sacramental seal. Whether the priest, bishop, or deacon is worthy or unworthy, Christ still acts through him. All the sacraments he celebrates are valid because it is Christ who effects them. It is Christ who is our one and only Priest, who is forever the one Mediator between God and us.

What does it mean to say that a priest shares in the one priesthood of Jesus Christ?

Jesus Christ, High Priest, source of all priesthood, stained glass

Bishops

A bishop receives the fullness of Holy Orders. Bishops are successors to the Apostles and share in the responsibility of service Christ gave to his Apostles. Appointed by the pope, the bishop is the visible head of a particular church entrusted to his care.

Priests

Priests in the Roman Catholic Church give themselves entirely to God and to the service of the Church by remaining celibate, or not marrying. Together with the bishop, priests form the presbyterium, or council of priests. They serve the people of the particular church of which the bishop serves as leader.

Priests are dependent upon the bishops for the exercise of their ministries of proclaiming and preaching the word of God, leading the faithful in worship, and guiding the faithful in living the Gospel. Priests receive their assignments from bishops and not from the people of the parishes they serve.

Deacons

Deacons carry out their work of service under the pastoral authority of the bishop. They assist bishops and priests at the celebration of Mass, in the distribution of Holy Communion, in blessing marriages, in the proclamation of the Gospel, in preaching, and in dedicating themselves to works of loving service.

FAITH CONNECTION

On the left is the motto of Blessed Pope John XXIII. In the space on the right create a motto that describes the work of the ordained ministry of the Church. Share your reasons for your motto with the class.

"Shepherd and Navigator"

OUR CHURCH
MAKES A DIFFERENCE

The Christian Family, the Domestic Church

The family is a sign of God's love. Pope John Paul II reminds us:

> The family has its origin in that same love with which the Creator embraces the created world. —LETTER TO FAMILIES

Children first hear God's invitation to trust in him in the experience of family members sharing their love for one another. They learn to live as children of God and eventually to share his love for them. The Christian family is "a community of grace and prayer, a school of human virtues and of Christian charity" (*Catechism of the Catholic Church* 1666). For this reason the Christian family is called a "domestic church," a "little church."

Christ gave his disciples the commandment to love one another as he loved them (see John 13:34–35). The Christian family is the first source of that love for its members. Sharing that love in word and action, one day at a time, helps prepare for the coming of the kingdom of God when the civilization of love first created by God will finally come about. Love is the foundation of civilization.

In what ways is your family a sign of God's love?

WHAT DIFFERENCE
Does Faith Make in My Life?

Love Begins at Home

In this chapter you have learned about the Sacraments at the Service of Communion and that the family is the domestic church. It is in our family that we first learn about God, values, and our religion. Through the love and service of family members for one another, we discover Christ's love for us.

As a member of a Christian family you are called to love your family and other people as Jesus did. Living the Spiritual Works of Mercy and the Corporal Works of Mercy enables you to reach out in love and service to your family and friends, and to your neighbors and to people all over the world.

Corporal Works of Mercy

Feed people who are hungry.

Give drink to people who are thirsty.

Clothe people who need clothes.

Visit prisoners.

Shelter people who are homeless.

Visit people who are sick.

Bury people who have died.

Spiritual Works of Mercy

Help people who sin.

Teach people who are ignorant.

Give advice to people who have doubts.

Comfort people who suffer.

Be patient with other people.

Forgive people who hurt you.

Pray for people who are alive and for those who have died.

Identify the work of mercy described in each item in this list. Then answer the questions.

❖ Your family feeds and nurtures you physically, spiritually, and emotionally.

What can you do to nourish your family?

How can you reach out to others beyond your family?

❖ Your family comforts and cares for you when you are sick, sad, or hurting physically, spiritually, and emotionally.

What can you do to comfort and care for your family?

How can you reach out to others beyond your family?

❖ Your family is patient with you and forgives you when you hurt them.

How can you practice patience and forgiveness in return?

How can you practice patience and forgiveness with people outside your family?

❖ Choose one other work of mercy.

What can you do to put it into practice in your family?

How can you practice it outside your family ?

Faith • Decision

• Role-play this situation. A TV producer is interviewing you for a new TV show about today's family values. Tell why your family should be selected.

• With a partner choose one of the works of mercy and discuss how living it can help the members of your family support and nourish one another.

This week I will choose one work of mercy and put it into action by

_____

_____

_____

_____

_____.

PRAY and REVIEW

Blessed Are God's People

The Beatitudes set before us the values and vision that are at the foundation of living the Gospel. They are the source of true happiness proclaimed and revealed in Jesus Christ.

Group 1:
Blessed are the poor in spirit,
All:
> **for theirs is the kingdom of heaven.**

Group 2:
Blessed are they who mourn,
All:
> **for they will be comforted.**

Group 1:
Blessed are the meek,
All:
> **for they will inherit the land.**

Group 2:
Blessed are they who hunger and thirst for righteousness,
All:
> **for they will be satisfied.**

Group 1:
Blessed are the merciful,
All:
> **for they will be shown mercy.**

Group 2:
Blessed are the clean of heart,
All:
> **for they will see God.**

Group 1:
Blessed are the peacemakers,
All:
> **for they will be called children of God.**

Group 2:
Blessed are they who are persecuted for the sake of righteousness,
All:
> **for theirs is the kingdom of heaven.**

(Share a sign of peace.)
BASED ON MATTHEW 5:3–10

FAITH VOCABULARY

Define each of these terms:

1. Sacraments at the Service of Communion
2. Matrimony
3. Holy Orders

MAIN IDEAS

Choose either (a) or (b) from each set of items. Write a brief paragraph to answer each of your choices.

1. (a) Name and explain the essential qualities of marriage.
   (b) Describe the effects on the lives of a baptized man and a baptized woman who celebrate the sacrament of Matrimony.

2. (a) Describe the essential elements of the rite of ordination.
   (b) Explain the role of bishops, priests, and deacons in the life of the Church.

CRITICAL THINKING

Using what you have learned in this chapter, reflect on and explain this statement:
> The Sacraments at the Service of Communion build up the Church on earth into the People of God.

FAMILY DISCUSSION

In what ways can the members of our family be signs of God's love?

For more ideas on ways your family can live your faith, visit the "Faith First for Families" page at **www.FaithFirst.com**. Also go to the Teen Center to find additional activities for this chapter.

UNIT TWO
REVIEWREVIEW

A. The Best Response

Read each statement and circle the best answer.

1. What are the Sacraments of Christian Initiation?
   A. Baptism, Confirmation, and Matrimony
   B. Baptism, Confirmation, and Holy Orders
   C. Baptism, Eucharist, and Holy Orders
   D. Baptism, Confirmation, and Eucharist

2. What does Baptism celebrate?
   A. We are joined to Christ.
   B. We become members of the Church.
   C. We receive the gift of the Holy Spirit.
   D. All of the above

3. Which of the following describes the sacrament of the Eucharist?
   A. We receive the Body and Blood of Christ.
   B. Jesus is present under the appearances of bread and wine.
   C. We are joined with Christ and give praise and thanksgiving to the Father.
   D. All of the above

4. In the sacrament of Anointing of the Sick we _____ .
   A. receive the grace to face illness with courage and strength
   B. receive forgiveness of original sin
   C. are anointed with chrism
   D. Both A and C

5. In the Sacraments at the Service of Communion _____ .
   A. a baptized man and a baptized woman become a sign of Christ's love for the Church
   B. a man is consecrated to serve the whole Church as a bishop, priest, or deacon
   C. a bishop is elected pope
   D. Both A and B

B. Matching Words and Phrases

Match the terms in column A with the descriptions in column B.

Column A

_____ 1. Paschal Mystery

_____ 2. grace

_____ 3. liturgical year

_____ 4. sacramentals

_____ 5. Blessed Sacrament

_____ 6. manna

_____ 7. conversion

_____ 8. seal of confession

_____ 9. priesthood of the faithful

_____ 10. ministerial priesthood

Column B

a. gift from God that makes us sharers of divine life

b. sacred signs such as the altar and blessings

c. breadlike food that the Israelites ate during the Exodus journey

d. turning our hearts toward God

e. conferred by the sacrament of Holy Orders

f. cycle of seasons and feasts the Church celebrates

g. absolute secrecy binding priests regarding sins confessed to them

h. Jesus' Passion, death, Resurrection, and Ascension

i. sharing by all the baptized in Christ's priestly ministry

j. the Eucharist reserved in the tabernacle

C. What I Have Learned

Using what you learned in this unit, write a two-sentence reflection about each of the following statements.

1. The Holy Spirit makes us sharers in God's life.

_____

_____

2. There are many graces of the sacrament of the Eucharist.

_____

_____

D. From a Scripture Story

On a separate sheet of paper do the following:

Describe how meeting with Jesus changed Nicodemus' life. Describe how your faith in Jesus and your meeting him in the sacraments changes your life.

Catholic Prayers and Practices

Sign of the Cross

In the name of the Father,
and of the Son,
and of the Holy Spirit. Amen.

Signum Crucis

In nómine Patris,
et Fílii,
et Spíritus Sancti. Amen.

Glory Be

Glory be to the Father
and to the Son
and to the Holy Spirit,
as it was in the beginning is now,
and ever shall be
world without end. Amen.

Gloria Patri

Glória Patri
et Fílio
et Spirítui Sancto.
Sicut erat in princípio,
et nunc et semper
et in sæcula sæculórum. Amen.

Lord's Prayer

Our Father, who art in heaven,
hallowed be thy name;
thy kingdom come,
thy will be done on earth
    as it is in heaven.
Give us this day our daily bread,
and forgive us our trespasses,
as we forgive those who trespass
    against us;
and lead us not into temptation,
but deliver us from evil. Amen.

Pater Noster

Pater noster, qui es in cælis:
sanctificétur nomen tuum;
advéniat regnum tuum;
fiat volúntas tua, sicut in cælo, et in terra.
Panem nostrum cotidiánum
    da nobis hódie;
et dimítte nobis débita nostra,
sicut et nos dimíttimus debitóribus nostris;
et ne nos indúcas in tentatiónem;
sed líbera nos a malo. Amen.

Hail Mary

Hail, Mary, full of grace,
the Lord is with thee.
Blessed art thou among women,
and blessed is the fruit
    of thy womb, Jesus.
Holy Mary, Mother of God,
pray for us sinners,
now and at the hour of our death.
Amen.

Ave, Maria

Ave, María, grátia plena,
Dóminus tecum.
Benedícta tu in muliéribus,
et benedíctus fructus ventris tui, Jesus.
Sancta María, Mater Dei,
ora pro nobis peccatóribus,
nunc et in hora mortis nostræ. Amen.

Nicene Creed

I believe in one God,
the Father almighty,
maker of heaven and earth,
of all things visible and invisible.

I believe in one Lord Jesus Christ,
the Only Begotten Son of God,
born of the Father before all ages.
God from God, Light from Light,
true God from true God,
begotten, not made, consubstantial
 with the Father;
through him all things were made.
For us men and for our salvation
he came down from heaven,
and by the Holy Spirit was incarnate
 of the Virgin Mary,
and became man.

For our sake he was crucified under
 Pontius Pilate,
he suffered death and was buried,
and rose again on the third day
in accordance with the Scriptures.
He ascended into heaven
and is seated at the right hand of the Father.
He will come again in glory
to judge the living and the dead
and his kingdom will have no end.

I believe in the Holy Spirit, the Lord,
 the giver of life,
who proceeds from the Father and the Son,
who with the Father and the Son
 is adored and glorified,
who has spoken through the prophets.

I believe in one, holy, catholic and
 apostolic Church.
I confess one Baptism for the forgiveness of sins
and I look forward to the resurrection of the dead
 and the life of the world to come.
Amen.

Apostles' Creed

I believe in God,
the Father almighty,
Creator of heaven and earth,
and in Jesus Christ, his only Son, our Lord,
who was conceived by the Holy Spirit,
born of the Virgin Mary,
suffered under Pontius Pilate,
was crucified, died and was buried;
he descended into hell;
on the third day he rose again from the dead;
he ascended into heaven,
and is seated at the right hand of God
 the Father almighty;
from there he will come to judge the living
 and the dead.

I believe in the Holy Spirit,
the holy catholic Church,
the communion of saints,
the forgiveness of sins,
the resurrection of the body,
and life everlasting. Amen.

Morning Prayer

Dear God,
as I begin this day,
keep me in your love and care.
Help me to live as your child today.
Bless me, my family, and my friends in all we do.
Keep us all close to you. Amen.

Evening Prayer

Dear God,
I thank you for today.
Keep me safe throughout the night.
Thank you for all the good I did today.
I am sorry for what I have chosen to do wrong.
Bless my family and friends. Amen.

Grace before Meals

Bless us, O Lord,
    and these thy gifts,
which we are about to receive
    from thy bounty,
through Christ our Lord. Amen.

Grace after Meals

We give thee thanks, for all thy benefits,
    almighty God,
who lives and reigns forever. Amen.

The Divine Praises

Blessed be God.
Blessed be his holy name.
Blessed be Jesus Christ, true God and true man.
Blessed be the name of Jesus.
Blessed be his most Sacred Heart.
Blessed be his most precious Blood.
Blessed be Jesus in the most holy Sacrament
    of the altar.
Blessed be the Holy Spirit, the Paraclete.
Blessed be the great Mother of God, Mary
    most holy.
Blessed be her holy and Immaculate
    Conception.
Blessed be her glorious Assumption.
Blessed be the name of Mary, Virgin and Mother.
Blessed be Saint Joseph, her most chaste spouse.
Blessed be God in his angels and in his saints.

Prayer to the Holy Spirit

Come, Holy Spirit, fill the hearts
    of your faithful.
And kindle in them the
    fire of your love.
Send forth your Spirit and
    they shall be created.
And you will renew the
    face of the earth.

Act of Faith

My God, I firmly believe that you are one God in three divine Persons, Father, Son, and Holy Spirit; I believe that your divine Son became man and died for our sins, and that he will come to judge the living and the dead. Amen.

Act of Hope

My God, relying on your infinite goodness and promises, I hope to obtain pardon of my sins, the help of your grace, and life everlasting, through the merits of Jesus Christ, my Lord and Redeemer. Amen.

Act of Love

My God, I love you above all things, with my whole heart and soul, because you are all good and worthy of all my love. I love my neighbor as myself for the love of you. I forgive all who have injured me and I ask pardon of all whom I have injured. Amen.

The Trinity,
stained glass

Magnificat

My soul proclaims the greatness
   of the Lord,
my spirit rejoices in God my Savior
for he has looked with favor
   on his lowly servant.

From this day all generations
   will call me blessed:
the Almighty has done great things
   for me,
and holy is his name.

He has mercy on those
   who fear him
in every generation.

He has shown the strength
   of his arm,
he has scattered the proud
   in their conceit.

He has cast down the mighty
   from their thrones,
and has lifted up the lowly.

He has filled the hungry
   with good things,
and the rich he has sent away empty.

He has come to the help
   of his servant Israel
for he has remembered
   his promise of mercy,
the promise he made to our fathers,
to Abraham and his children for ever.

BASED ON LUKE 1:46–55
FROM CATHOLIC HOUSEHOLD BLESSINGS AND PRAYERS

Memorare

Remember, O most gracious Virgin Mary,
that never was it known
that anyone who fled to your protection,
implored your help,
or sought your intercession was left unaided.

Inspired by this confidence,
I fly unto you, O Virgin of virgins, my mother;
to you do I come,
before you I stand, sinful and sorrowful.

O Mother of the Word Incarnate,
despise not my petitions,
but in your mercy
   hear and answer me.
Amen.

Our Lady
of the
Rosary

Rosary

Catholics pray the Rosary to honor Mary and remember the important events in the life of Jesus and Mary. We begin praying the Rosary by praying the Apostles' Creed, the Lord's Prayer, and three Hail Marys. Each mystery of the Rosary is prayed by praying the Lord's Prayer once, the Hail Mary ten times, and the Glory Be once. When we have finished the last mystery, we pray the Hail, Holy Queen.

Joyful Mysteries

1. The Annunciation
2. The Visitation
3. The Nativity
4. The Presentation in the Temple
5. The Finding of the Child Jesus After Three Days in the Temple

Luminous Mysteries

1. The Baptism at the Jordan
2. The Miracle at Cana
3. The Proclamation of the Kingdom and the Call to Conversion
4. The Transfiguration
5. The Institution of the Eucharist

Sorrowful Mysteries

1. The Agony in the Garden
2. The Scourging at the Pillar
3. The Crowning with Thorns
4. The Carrying of the Cross
5. The Crucifixion and Death

Glorious Mysteries

1. The Resurrection
2. The Ascension
3. The Descent of the Holy Spirit at Pentecost
4. The Assumption of Mary
5. The Crowning of the Blessed Virgin as Queen of Heaven and Earth

Hail, Holy Queen

Hail, holy Queen, Mother of mercy:
Hail, our life, our sweetness
    and our hope.
To you do we cry, poor banished children of Eve.
To you do we send up our sighs,
mourning and weeping
    in this valley of tears.
Turn then, most gracious advocate,
your eyes of mercy toward us;
and after this our exile
show unto us the blessed fruit
    of your womb, Jesus.
O clement, O loving, O sweet
    Virgin Mary.

Stations of the Cross

1. Jesus is condemned to death.

2. Jesus accepts his cross.

3. Jesus falls the first time.

4. Jesus meets his mother.

5. Simon helps Jesus carry the cross.

6. Veronica wipes the face of Jesus.

7. Jesus falls the second time.

8. Jesus meets the women.

9. Jesus falls the third time.

10. Jesus is stripped of his clothes.

11. Jesus is nailed to the cross.

12. Jesus dies on the cross.

13. Jesus is taken down from the cross.

14. Jesus is buried in the tomb.

Some parishes conclude the Stations by reflecting on the Resurrection of Jesus.

The Great Commandment

"You shall love the Lord,
your God, with all your
heart, with all your soul,
and with all your mind. . . .
You shall love your neighbor as yourself."

MATTHEW 22:37, 39

The Ten Commandments

1. I am the LORD your God: you shall not have strange gods before me.
2. You shall not take the name of the LORD your God in vain.
3. Remember to keep holy the LORD's Day.
4. Honor your father and your mother.
5. You shall not kill.
6. You shall not commit adultery.
7. You shall not steal.
8. You shall not bear false witness against your neighbor.
9. You shall not covet your neighbor's wife.
10. You shall not covet your neighbor's goods.

Precepts of the Church

1. Participate in Mass on Sundays and holy days of obligation and rest from unnecessary work.
2. Confess sins at least once a year.
3. Receive Holy Communion at least during the Easter season.
4. Observe the prescribed days of fasting and abstinence.
5. Provide for the material needs of the Church, according to one's abilities.

The Beatitudes

"Blessed are the poor in spirit,
for theirs is the kingdom of heaven.
Blessed are they who mourn,
for they will be comforted.
Blessed are the meek,
for they will inherit the land.
Blessed are they who hunger
and thirst for righteousness,
for they will be satisfied.
Blessed are the merciful,
for they will be shown mercy.
Blessed are the clean of heart,
for they will see God.
Blessed are the peacemakers,
for they will be called children of God.
Blessed are they who are persecuted for the
sake of righteousness,
for theirs is the kingdom of heaven.

"Blessed are you when they insult you and persecute you and utter every kind of evil against you [falsely] because of me. Rejoice and be glad, for your reward will be great in heaven."

MATTHEW 5:3–12

The Beatitude Window,
stained glass.
Jerry Sodorff, artist.

Theological Virtues

Faith
Hope
Love

Cardinal, or Moral, Virtues

Prudence
Justice
Fortitude
Temperance

Corporal Works of Mercy

Feed people who are hungry.
Give drink to people who are thirsty.
Clothe people who need clothes.
Visit prisoners.
Shelter people who are homeless.
Visit people who are sick.
Bury people who have died.

Spiritual Works of Mercy

Help people who sin.
Teach people who are ignorant.
Give advice to people who have doubts.
Comfort people who suffer.
Be patient with other people.
Forgive people who hurt you.
Pray for people who are alive and
    for those who have died.

Gifts of the Holy Spirit

Wisdom
Understanding
Right judgment (Counsel)
Courage (Fortitude)
Knowledge
Reverence (Piety)
Wonder and awe (Fear of the Lord)

Fruits of the Holy Spirit

Love
Joy
Peace
Patience
Kindness
Goodness
Generosity
Gentleness
Faithfulness
Modesty
Self-control
Chastity

Faith, Hope, and Charity, stained glass

Basic Principles of the Church's Teaching on Social Justice

The Church's teaching on social justice guides us in living lives of holiness and building a just society. These principles are:

1. All human life is sacred. The basic equality of all people flows from their dignity as human persons and the rights that flow from that dignity.

2. The human person is the principle, the object, and the subject of every social group.

3. The human person has been created by God to belong to and to participate in a family and other social communities.

4. Respect for the rights of people flows from their dignity as persons. Society and all social organizations must promote virtue and protect human life and human rights and guarantee the conditions that promote the exercise of freedom.

5. Political communities and public authority are based on human nature. They belong to an order established by God.

6. All human authority must be used for the common good of society.

7. The common good of society consists of respect for and promotion of the fundamental rights of the human person; the just development of material and spiritual goods of society; and the peace and safety of all people.

8. We need to work to eliminate the sinful inequalities that exist between peoples and for the improvement of the living conditions of people. The needs of the poor and vulnerable have a priority.

9. We are one human and global family. We are to share our spiritual blessings, even more than our material blessings.

Based on the *Catechism of the Catholic Church*

143

The Seven Sacraments

Jesus gave the Church the seven sacraments. The sacraments are the main liturgical signs of the Church. They make the Paschal Mystery of Jesus, who is always the main celebrant of each sacrament, present to us. They make us sharers in the saving work of Christ and in the life of the Holy Trinity.

Sacraments of Initiation

Baptism
We are joined to Jesus Christ, become members of the Church, receive the gift of the Holy Spirit, and are reborn as God's adopted children. Original and all personal sins are forgiven.

Confirmation
Our Baptism is sealed with the gift of the Holy Spirit.

Eucharist
We receive the Body and Blood of Christ who is truly and really present under the appearances of bread and wine. We share in the one sacrifice of Christ. Sharing in the Eucharist most fully joins us to Christ and to the Church.

Sacraments of Healing

Penance and Reconciliation
We receive God's gift of forgiveness and peace.

Anointing of the Sick
Jesus' work of healing is continued in our lives and strengthens our faith and trust in God when we are seriously ill or dying.

Sacraments at the Service of Communion

Holy Orders
A baptized man is ordained and consecrated to serve the Church as a bishop, priest, or deacon.

Matrimony
A baptized man and a baptized woman are united in a lifelong bond of faithful love. They become a sign of God's love for all people and of Christ's love for the Church.

Baptism   Eucharist   Confirmation   Matrimony

Penance and Reconciliation   Holy Orders   Anointing of the Sick

Celebrating the Mass

The Introductory Rites

The Entrance
Sign of the Cross
  and Greeting
The Penitential Act
The Gloria
The Collect

The Liturgy of the Word

The First Reading
  (Usually from the
  Old Testament)
The Psalm
The Second Reading
  (Usually from New
  Testament Letters)
The Gospel Acclamation
The Gospel
The Homily
The Profession of Faith
Prayer of the Faithful

The Liturgy of the Eucharist

The Preparation of the Gifts
The Prayer over the Offerings
The Eucharistic Prayer
The Communion Rite
  The Lord's Prayer
  The Sign of Peace
  The Fraction
  Communion
The Prayer After Communion

The Concluding Rites

The Greeting
The Blessing
The Dismissal

Celebrating Penance and Reconciliation

Individual Rite of Reconciliation

Greeting

Scripture Reading

Confession of Sins

Act of Contrition

Absolution

Closing Prayer

Communal Rite of Reconciliation

Greeting

Scripture Reading

Homily

Examination of Conscience with Litany of
  Contrition and the Lord's Prayer

Individual Confession and Absolution

Closing Prayer

Act of Contrition

My God,
I am sorry for my sins with all my heart.
In choosing to do wrong
and failing to do good,
I have sinned against you
whom I should love above all things.
I firmly intend, with your help,
to do penance,
to sin no more,
and to avoid whatever leads me to sin.
Our Savior Jesus Christ
suffered and died for us.
In his name, my God, have mercy.

The Books of the Bible

The Old Testament

Law (Torah) or Pentateuch

Genesis	(Gn)
Exodus	(Ex)
Leviticus	(Lv)
Numbers	(Nm)
Deuteronomy	(Dt)

Historical Books

Joshua	(Jos)
Judges	(Jgs)
Ruth	(Ru)
First Book of Samuel	(1 Sm)
Second Book of Samuel	(2 Sm)
First Book of Kings	(1 Kgs)
Second Book of Kings	(2 Kgs)
First Book of Chronicles	(1 Chr)
Second Book of Chronicles	(2 Chr)
Ezra	(Ezr)
Nehemiah	(Neh)
Tobit	(Tb)
Judith	(Jdt)
Esther	(Est)
First Book of Maccabees	(1 Mc)
Second Book of Maccabees	(2 Mc)

The Poetry and Wisdom Books

Job	(Jb)
Psalms	(Ps)
Proverbs	(Prv)
Ecclesiastes	(Eccl)
Song of Songs	(Sg)
Wisdom	(Wis)
Sirach/Ecclesiasticus	(Sir)

Prophets

Isaiah	(Is)
Jeremiah	(Jer)
Lamentations	(Lam)
Baruch	(Bar)
Ezekiel	(Ez)
Daniel	(Dn)
Hosea	(Hos)
Joel	(Jl)
Amos	(Am)
Obadiah	(Ob)
Jonah	(Jon)
Micah	(Mi)
Nahum	(Na)
Habakkuk	(Hb)
Zephaniah	(Zep)
Haggai	(Hg)
Zechariah	(Zec)
Malachi	(Mal)

The New Testament

The Gospels

Matthew	(Mt)
Mark	(Mk)
Luke	(Lk)
John	(Jn)

Early Church

Acts of the Apostles	(Acts)

Letters of Paul and Other Letters

Romans	(Rom)
First Letter to the Corinthians	(1 Cor)
Second Letter to the Corinthians	(2 Cor)
Galatians	(Gal)
Ephesians	(Eph)
Philippians	(Phil)
Colossians	(Col)
First Letter to the Thessalonians	(1 Thes)
Second Letter to the Thessalonians	(2 Thes)
First Letter to Timothy	(1 Tm)
Second Letter to Timothy	(2 Tm)
Titus	(Ti)
Philemon	(Phlm)
Hebrews	(Heb)
James	(Jas)
First Letter of Peter	(1 Pt)
Second Letter of Peter	(2 Pt)
First Letter of John	(1 Jn)
Second Letter of John	(2 Jn)
Third Letter of John	(3 Jn)
Jude	(Jude)

Revelation

Revelation	(Rv)

Glossary

A-B

Acts of the Apostles
New Testament book written by Saint Luke which continues the narrative of the Gospel according to Luke passing on the proclamation of the Gospel from the time of the Resurrection to Saint Paul's preaching in Rome.

actual grace
God-given divine help empowering us to live as his adopted daughters and sons.

Anointing of the Sick
A Sacrament of Healing. This sacrament confers the grace of strengthening our faith and trust in God when we are seriously ill, weakened by old age, or dying.

apostolic succession
The unbroken connection between the popes and bishops with the Apostles; bishops are the successors of the Apostles.

Baptism
The sacrament by which we are reborn into new life in Christ. The sacrament in which we are joined to Jesus Christ, become members of the Church, and are reborn as God's children. We receive the gift of the Holy Spirit, and original sin and our personal sins are forgiven.

Beatitudes
Part of the Sermon on the Mount. The statements in the Gospel that begin with the phrase "Blessed are . . ." that describe the happiness of those who keep their life focused and centered on God. The sayings or teachings of Jesus that describe the qualities and actions of people blessed by God. The word *beatitude* means "blessing" or "happiness."

Blessed Sacrament
The Eucharist reserved in the tabernacle.

Body of Christ
A New Testament image for the Church used by Saint Paul the Apostle that teaches that all the members of the Church are one in Christ, the Head of the Church, and that all members of the Body of Christ have a unique and important role in the work of the Church.

C-D

Church
The word *church* means "convocation, those called together." Church is the sacrament of salvation—the sign and instrument of our reconciliation and communion with God and one another. The Body of Christ; the people God the Father has called together in Jesus Christ through the power of the Holy Spirit.

Communion of Saints
All the faithful followers of Jesus Christ, both the living and the dead; the communion of holy things and holy people that make up the Church.

Confirmation
The sacrament that strengthens the graces of Baptism and that celebrates the special gift of the Holy Spirit.

consecrated life
The life of the baptized who promise or vow to live the Gospel counsels of poverty, chastity, and obedience in a way of life approved by the Church.

contemplation
A form of prayer that is simply being with God.

conversion
A renewal of our friendship with God and the Church; turning our hearts back to God's love and away from choices that weaken our friendship with God.

deposit of faith
The source of faith that is drawn from to pass on God's revelation to us; it is the unity of Scripture and Tradition.

devotions
Acts of individual or communal prayer that surround and arise out of the celebration of the liturgy.

disciple
The follower of a teacher. In Christianity, a follower of Jesus; one who places total, unconditional trust in God the Father, as Jesus did—and in no one and nothing else.

divine Providence
God's caring love for us. The attribute of God that his almighty power and caring love is always with us.

E-F

ecumenism
The dedicated search to draw all Christians together to manifest the unity that Christ wills for his Body, the Church, on earth.

eternal life
Life after death; "the life everlasting" (Apostles' Creed); "the life of the world to come" (Nicene Creed).

Eucharist
The sacrament in which we share in the Paschal Mystery of Christ and receive the Body and Blood of Christ, who is truly present under the appearances of bread and wine. The word *eucharist* is from a Greek word meaning "thanksgiving" or "gratitude."

Evangelists
Inspired writers of the Gospel: Matthew, Mark, Luke, and John.

evangelize
To proclaim the Gospel.

Glossary

Exodus

The saving intervention of God in the history of God's people, the Israelites—the saving of the Israelites from slavery in Egypt, God's making of the Covenant with them, and God's leading them to freedom in the land he promised them.

G

Gentiles

The biblical reference to those who are not Jewish.

grace

The gift of our sharing in God's life.

H

heresies

Religious opinions contrary to the teachings of the Apostles and the Church.

holiness

Living our life in Christ; the characteristic of a person who is in right relationship with God. Holiness refers to God's presence with us and our faithfulness to God.

Holy Orders

The sacrament of the Church that consecrates baptized men as bishops, priests, or deacons to serve the whole Church in the name and person of Christ by teaching, divine worship, and governing the Church as Jesus did.

I-J-K-L

icons

Pictures or images of Christ, Mary, a saint, or an angel.

idols

False gods; anything that takes the place of God in our life.

infallibility

The charism of the Holy Spirit given to the Church that guarantees that the official teaching of the pope, or pope and bishops, on matters of faith and morals is without error.

intellect

The power to know God, ourselves, and others; the power to reflect on how God is part of our lives.

Jerusalem

The political and religious center of the Israelite people.

justification

The gift of new life in Christ that we receive at Baptism through sanctifying grace.

laypeople

All the baptized who have not received the sacrament of Holy Orders nor promised or vowed to live the consecrated life.

liturgical year

The cycle of seasons and feasts that make up the Church's year of worship.

liturgy

The Church's worship of God.

M-N

Magisterium

The teaching authority and office of the Church, guided by the Holy Spirit, to authentically and accurately interpret the word of God, Scripture and Tradition.

manna

The breadlike substance the Israelites ate during their Exodus journey through the desert.

Marks of the Church

One, holy, catholic, and apostolic; the four attributes and essential characteristics of the Church and of the mission of the Church.

martyrs

Heroic figures who give their lives for their faith in Christ.

Matrimony

The sacrament of the Church that consecrates a baptized man and a baptized woman in a lifelong bond of faithful love as a living sign of Christ's love for the Church.

meditation

A form of prayer using our minds, hearts, imaginations, emotions, and desires to understand and follow what the Lord is asking us to do.

memorial

A term used by the Church to signify that the Eucharist *makes present* and does not simply recall the past events of Christ's Paschal Mystery.

missionary

A Christian who travels to places in their own country and in other countries to live and preach the Gospel.

monasticism

A way of living the Gospel; men and women living in community who devote themselves to prayer, work, and learning.

O-P-Q

ordained ministry

The ministry of bishops, priests, and deacons.

order

The office in which one has a sacred duty to serve the Church. When a baptized man receives the sacrament of Holy Orders, he becomes a member of the order of bishops, priests, or deacons.

Paschal Mystery
The saving events of the Passion, death, Resurrection, and glorious Ascension of Jesus Christ; the passing over of Jesus from death into a new and glorious life; the name we give to God's plan of saving us in Jesus Christ.

Pharisees
A lay sect within Judaism whose members have dedicated their lives to the strict keeping of the Law found in the Torah.

prayer
Conversation with God; talking and listening to God; raising our minds and hearts to God, who is Father, Son, and Holy Spirit.

presbyters
Leaders in the early Church chosen by the Apostles.

R

rabbi
A teacher of the Law.

Reconciliation
The sacrament through which we receive forgiveness of sins by the sincere confessing of our sins to a priest to whom the power to forgive sins has been given.

reverence
The attitude of awe, profound respect, and love.

rites
The words and actions used to celebrate the liturgy.

S

sacramentals
Sacred signs instituted by the Church. They include blessings, prayers, and certain objects that prepare us to participate in the sacraments and make us aware of and help us respond to God's loving presence in our lives.

sacraments
Effective signs of grace, instituted by Christ and entrusted to the Church, by which divine life is shared with us; the seven main liturgical actions of the Church.

Sacraments at the Service of Communion
Holy Orders and Matrimony.

Sacraments of Christian Initiation
Baptism, Confirmation, and Eucharist.

Sacraments of Healing
Anointing of the Sick and Reconciliation (or Penance).

sacrifice
The free offering out of love of something of great value, for example, one's life.

sanctification
The work of the Holy Spirit that unites us by faith and Baptism to the Passion and Resurrection of Christ. We become sharers of God's life through the work of the Holy Spirit.

sanctifying grace
God sharing his life and love with us; the gift of God's life and love that makes us holy.

Sanhedrin
The supreme governing council of the Jewish people during Jesus' time.

sin
Freely and knowingly doing or saying what we know is against God's Law. Sin sets itself against God's love for us and turns our hearts away from God's love.

soul
The spiritual part of who we are that is immortal and never dies; our innermost being; that which bears the imprint of the image of God.

stewardship
The managing and caring for the property of another person. We are called to be stewards of God's creation.

symbols
Signs or actions that point to something much deeper than first meets the eye.

T-U

Temple of the Holy Spirit
New Testament image used to describe the indwelling of the Holy Spirit in the Church and within the hearts of the faithful.

theological virtues
Faith, hope, and charity—strengths or habits that God gives us to help us attain holiness.

Torah
The Law of God revealed to Moses, which is found in the first five books of the Old Testament.

V-W-X-Y-Z

vernacular
The common language used by people.

virtues
Spiritual powers or habits or behaviors that help us do what is right and avoid what is wrong.

vocal prayer
Spoken prayer; prayer using words said aloud or in the quiet of one's heart.

worship
To honor and respect God above all else.

Index

Credits

Cover Design: Kristy Howard
Cover Illustration: Amy Freeman

PHOTO AND ART CREDITS:
Abbreviated as follows: (bkgd) background;
(t) top; (b) bottom; (l) left; (r) right;
(c) center.

Frontmatter: Page 5, © PhotoDisc/Punchstock; 6, © Dream Stock/Index Stock; 7 (t), © Myrleen Cate/Index Stock; 7 (cr, b), © The Crosiers/Gene Plaisted, OSC; 8, © North Carolina Museum of Art/Corbis.

Chapter 1: Page 9, © Bill Wittman; 10, © The Crosiers/Gene Plaisted, OSC; 11, © Bill Wittman; 12 (t), © Mary Kate Denny/Photoeditinc; 12 (b), © Bill Wittman; 13 (t), © Myrleen Cate/Index Stock; 13 (c), © Michael St. Maur Sheil/Corbis; 13 (b), © Mark Gibson/Index Stock; 14, © James L. Shaffer; 15 (t), © Bettman/Corbis; 15 (c, b), © F. Lochon/Gamma; 16 (t), © Mitch Wojnarowicz/The Image Works; 16 (c), © Rob Lewine/Corbis; 16 (bl), © Will Hart/Photoeditinc; 16 (br), 17, © Myrleen Ferguson Cate/Photoeditinc.

Chapter 2: Page 19, © Diana Ong/SuperStock; 20 (Bkgd), © Matthias Kulka/Corbis; 20 (t), © Tony Freeman/Photoeditinc; 20 (c), © Jeff Greenberg/Photoeditinc; 20 (b), © Jonathan Nourok/Photoeditinc; 21 (t), © Diana Ong/SuperStock; 22 (l), © Reuters/Corbis; 22 (r), © Arturo Mari/L'Osservatore Romano/Citta del Vaticano/Servicio/Fotografico; 23 (t), © Pizzoli Alberto/Corbis; 23 (b), © Joe Sohm/Stock, Boston/Picturequest; 24, © Vicenzo Pinto/AP/Wide World Photos; 25 (l), © Myrleen Cate/Index Stock; 25 (r), © Bill Wittman; 26 (c), © Tony Freeman/Photoeditinc; 26 (bl), © Ariel Skelley/Corbis; 26 (br), © David Young-Wolff/Photoeditinc; 27 (t, c), © Bill Wittman; 27 (b), © Michael Pole/Corbis.

Chapter 3: Page 29, © The Crosiers/Gene Plaisted, OSC; 30 (all), © Bill Alger; 31, © North Carolina Museum of Art/Corbis; 32 (all), © The Crosiers/Gene Plaisted, OSC; 33, © Allen Jacobs Gallery/London/Bridgeman Art Library; 34 (t), © Jim McDonald/Corbis; 34 (c), © AP/Wide World Photos; 35 (t, br), Courtesy of Anne, Lisa, Laura & Leslie Parker; 35 (l), Courtesy of Mary Beth Jambor; 36, 37, © David Young-Wolff/Photoeditinc.

Chapter 4: Page 39, © Myrleen Ferguson Cate/Photoeditinc; 40 (all), © Bill Wittman; 41 (t), © Jeff Greenberg/Photoeditinc; 41 (c), © Tony Freeman/Photoeditinc; 41 (b), © Bill Wittman; 42 (t), © Steve Skjold/Photoeditinc; 42 (bl, br), © Bill Wittman; 43, © The Crosiers/Gene Plaisted, OSC, 44, © Corbis/Punchstock; 45, © Bill Wittman; 46, © Jeanene Tiner; 47 (t), © Myrleen Ferguson Cate/Photoeditinc; 47 (b), © SW Production/Index Stock;

Chapter 5: Page 49, © The Crosiers/Gene Plaisted, OSC; 50 (t), © Myrleen Ferguson Cate/Photoeditinc; 50 (b), © Bill Wittman; 51, © Morry Gash/AP/Wide World Photos; 52, © Bill Wittman; 53, © Jose Ortega/Images.com; 54 (t), © Cindy Charles/Photoeditinc; 54 (b), © Spencer Grant/Photoeditinc; 55 (t), © Bonnie Kamin/Photoeditinc; 55 (c), © Ted Streshinsky/Corbis; 55 (b), Courtesy of the Poor Clare Nuns, Jamaica Plain, MA; 56 (t), © David Young-Wolff/Photoeditinc; 56 (b), © Gettyimages/Punchstock; 57, © David Young-Wolff/Photoeditinc; 61 (t, b), © The Crosiers/Gene Plaisted, OSC; 61 (c), © Paul Aresu/FPG International; 62, © James Tissot/SuperStock.

Chapter 6: Page 63, 64, 65 (t), © The Crosiers/Gene Plaisted, OSC; 65 (b), © Bill Wittman; 66-67 (all), 68, © The Crosiers/Gene Plaisted, OSC; 69 (t), Courtesy of the Sisters of Mercy; 69 (bl), © Philip Gould/Corbis; 69 (br), © Martin Mejia/AP/Wide World Photos; 70, © LWA-Stephen Welstead/Corbis; 71, © Larry Dale Gordon/Gettyimages.

Chapter 7: Page 73, © The Crosiers/Gene Plaisted, OSC; 74, © James Tissot/SuperStock; 75, © Corbis/Punchstock; 76, © James Tissot/SuperStock; 77, © Steve Satushek/Gettyimages; 78, © Lonnie Duka/PictureQuest; 79 (t, c, bl), © Bill Wittman; 79 (br), © The Crosiers/Gene Plaisted, OSC; 80, © Dale O'Dell/Images.com; 81 (t), © Nancy Tolford/Images.com.

Chapter 8: Page 83, 84 (all), 85 (all), © The Crosiers/Gene Plaisted, OSC; 86, 87, © Bill Wittman; 88, © The Crosiers/Gene Plaisted, OSC; 89, © John LeMay/National Federation for Catholic Youth Ministry; 90 (l), © Charles Gupton/Corbis; 90 (r), © Tom Stewart/Corbis; 91 (t), © Gettyimages/Punchstock; 91 (b), © Omni Photo Communications, Inc./PictureQuest.

Chapter 9: Page 93, © The Crosiers/Gene Plaisted, OSC; 94, © Andy Zito/Images.com; 95, © Bill Wittman; 96, © Myrleen Ferguson Cate/Photoeditinc; 97, © Bill Wittman; 99 (bkgd), © Corbis/Punchstock; 99 (br), Courtesy of Bread for the World; 100–101, © Tom Stewart/Corbis.

Chapter 10: Page 103, © Pier Paolo Cito/AP/Wide World Photos; 104 (l), © Bridgeman Art Gallery; 104 (r), © James Tissot/SuperStock; 105 (bkgd), Amy Freeman; 105, © Rene-Marie Castaing/Bridgeman Art Library; 106 (l), © Laura James/Bridgeman Art Gallery; 106 (r), © Michael Wolgemuth/Bridgeman Art Gallery; 107, © James Tissot/SuperStock; 108 (t), © Tony Freeman/Photoeditinc; 109 (t), © Jeff Greenberg/Photoeditinc; 109 (b), Courtesy of St. Mark the Evangelist Catholic Church, Plano, Texas; 110–111 (bkgd), © Kristen Miller/Images.com; 110 (tl), © Bill Wittman; 110 (tr), © Michael Newman/Photoeditinc; 110 (b), © Arthur Tilley/Gettyimages.

Chapter 11: Page 113, © Paul Aresu/FPG International; 114, © The Crosiers/Gene Plaisted, OSC; 115 (t), © Alan Oddie/Photoeditinc; 115 (b), © Bill Wittman; 116, © Ghislain & Marie David deLassy/Gettyimages; 117 (all), © Myrleen Ferguson Cate/Photoeditinc; 118 (t), © The Crosiers/Gene Plaisted, OSC; 118 (b), © John Giustina/Gettyimages; 121 (t), © Ron Chapple/Gettyimages; 119 (bl), © Joseph Nettis/Stock, Boston; 119 (br), © Myrleen Ferguson Cate/Photoeditinc; 120, © Todd Davidson/Images.com; 121 (t), © Tony Freeman; 121 (b), © David R. Frazier/The Image Works.

Chapter 12: Page 123, © Gettyimages/Punchstock; 124 (c), © Roy Morsch/Corbis; 124 (t), © Spencer Grant/Photoeditinc; 124 (b), © Gettyimages/Punchstock; 125, 126 (all), 127, © The Crosiers/Gene Plaisted, OSC; 128 (t), © Bill Wittman; 128 (c, b), © The Crosiers/Gene Plaisted, OSC; 129 (t), © Philip Lee Harvey/Gettyimages; 129 (r), © Gettyimages/Punchstock; 129 (b), © Ronnie Kaufman/Corbis; 130 (t), © Joe Carini/PictureQuest; 130 (c), © Tony Freeman/Photoeditinc; 131 (t), © Robert Brenner/Photoeditinc; 131 (b), © Paul Barton/Corbis.

Backmatter: Page 135, © The Crosiers/Gene Plaisted, OSC; 136, © Bill Wittman; 137, 138, 139, © The Crosiers/Gene Plaisted, OSC; 140, drawings by Angela Marina Barbieri & Joan Lledô Vila; 141, © Jerry Sodorff/The Spirit Source; 142, 143, 144, 145 (all), 146, The Crosiers/Gene Plaisted, OSC.

CPSIA information can be obtained
at www.ICGtesting.com
Printed in the USA
LVHW051655300622
722437LV00002B/29